X Listed

PARAGUAY

PARAGUAY

A RIVERSIDE NATION

by

GEORGE PENDLE

Le nom 'Guarani' qui signifie
'guerrier' . . . était bien mérité.

C. LUGON

THIRD EDITION

Issued under the auspices of the
Royal Institute of International Affairs

OXFORD UNIVERSITY PRESS

LONDON   NEW YORK   TORONTO

1967

First published 1954
Second edition 1956
Third edition 1967

PRINTED IN GREAT BRITAIN

PREFACE TO THIRD EDITION

THERE is a remarkable consistency in the story of Paraguay. Century after century the same characteristics reappear. History may not repeat itself, but geographical factors remain constant; and to an extraordinary degree the history of Paraguay has been shaped by geography.

Paraguayans feel that their national problems today are essentially the same as they have been for four centuries. In this study, therefore, more space is devoted to the historical background than, in other circumstances, would be necessary. The past not only helps to explain the present but seems to be very much a part of it—a recent traveller, Gordon Meyer, frequently had the impression that Marshal López and his Madama (the two leading figures in Paraguay's tragic war of 1865–70) were, even now, just there, at hand: 'a door is heard opening, a step behind one, one looks up, a little uneasily it is confessed, half expecting to be surprised by him, to see that heavy sensual face, the thick luxuriant black beard, the burning eyes, and then to hear the rustle of a dress, as she follows'.

Contemporary events often seem to be a repetition, *mutatis mutandis*, of what has gone before. Even the physical appearance of the country and the towns has altered much less than is usual.

Paraguayan friends were displeased because in the Preface to the second edition of this book I wrote that, when re-visiting Asunción in 1955, I was enchanted to find that almost nothing had changed since I was there in the 1940s—the trees in the garden of H.M. Embassy were taller than before; a few higher buildings had been erected in the centre of the town; and the petroleum storage tanks had been completed by Shell. But the sun still blazed on red dust streets; the sweet perfume of tropical flowers and fruits was still in the air; dark-eyed, straight-backed women with bare feet walked home from the river with bundles of white laundry on their heads. I was told that a revolution was expected 'any day now'; and it was evident that the young conscripts who lolled in faded cotton uniforms at General Staff Headquarters had no idea whether they would be summoned next to defend, or to overthrow, the Government of the day.

Ten years later I found, to my renewed delight, that nothing of

v

any importance had changed in Asunción—true, there was an exceptionally stable Government, a new hotel. Outside town, new roads now reached Brazil and the frontier of Bolivia, but they had not yet had any very noticeable effect on the regions through which they passed.

For assistance in preparing this third edition I am indebted to my old friend Don Federico Hewitt. I tracked down Don Federico to a building near the port at Asunción: he stood to receive me (he was suffering terribly from arthritis) in a dark, high-ceilinged room—the *persianas* were closed, to keep out the glare of the sun. Dr Francia, the Parish Robertsons, López, Madama—they would all have found themselves perfectly at home in this dark, quiet room; we could have discussed together (almost ignoring the interval of so many years) the state of the *yerba* market, the extent of the seasonal fall in the level of the river, the pretensions and rivalries of the Argentines and Brazilians, the desirability of strong personal government. . . .

I thank Rupert Baldock for his advice and for sending to me, from Asunción, the latest official publications and statistics.

The extent of my debt to Katharine Duff can only be appreciated by authors whose books have had the benefit of her scrupulous editing.

September 1966   G. P.

CONTENTS

vii

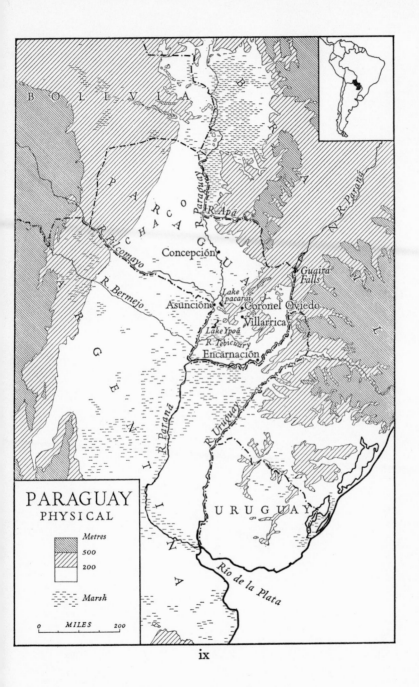

PARAGUAY
PHYSICAL

Metres
500
200

Marsh

0   MILES   200

BOLIVIA

P A R A G U A Y

C H A C O

R. Pilcomayo

R. Bermejo

A R G E N T I N A

Concepción

Asunción

Lake
Ypacarai

Lake Ypoá

R. Tebicuary

Encarnación

R. Paraná

R. Paraguay

R. Apa

Coronel Oviedo

Villarrica

Guaira
Falls

B R A Z I L

R. Paraná

Uruguay

U R U G U A Y

R. Uruguay

Río de la Plata

ix

Chapter I

THE PLATEAU AND THE CHACO

FOR many centuries Europeans have imagined Paradise as a green landscape full of flowers, fruits, and birds, a garden of perpetual spring.[1] Just such a country was the eastern region of Paraguay which the Spaniards, exploring upstream from the Plata estuary, entered early in the sixteenth century; and countless later travellers have described this land as an Arcadia. Voltaire had heard of it and sent his Candide thither in search of happiness. In 1811 a young Scottish merchant, coming from Argentina, was delighted with the idyllic scene:

> ... I soon recognized a striking difference between the character of the country in which I now was, and that of any part over which I had hitherto travelled. The open pampa was exchanged for the shady grove; the pastures, protected by the trees, and irrigated by abundant streams, were in most places beautifully green; the palm-tree was a frequent occupant of the plain; hills, and more gently sloping eminences, contrasted beautifully with the valley and the lake. Wooded from the base to the top, those hills and slopes exhibited now the stately forest-tree, and anon the less-aspiring shrub, the lime and the orange, each bearing, at the same time, both blossom and fruit. The fig-tree spread its broad dark leaf, and offered its delicious fruit to the traveller without money and without price; while the parasite plant lent all its variety of leaf and flower to adorn the scene. Pendent from the boughs of many of the trees was to be seen, and yet more distinctly known by its fragrance, the air-plant. Squirrels leaped, and monkeys chattered among the branches; the parrot and the parroquet, the pheasant, the moigtû, the toucan, the humming-bird, the guacamayo or cockatoo, and innumerable others ... inhabited, in all their gaudy variety of plumage, the woods through which I rode.[2]

As far as eastern Paraguay is concerned, the Scotsman's picture is still true today. This eastern region of the republic varies from 1,000 to 2,000 feet in altitude and is an extension of the plateau of southern Brazil. It is bounded on the south-east by the

[1] Pedro Henríquez-Ureña, *Literary Currents in Hispanic America* (Cambridge, Mass., Harvard University Press, 1949), p. 9.

[2] J. P. and W. P. Robertson, *Letters on Paraguay* (London, Murray, 1838), vol. 1, pp. 259–60.

I

Río Paraná, which drops spectacularly in the Guairá Falls at the most easterly point in the Paraguayan-Brazilian frontier. Between the Guairá Falls and the confluence with the Río Paraguay, the Paraná flows through a deep canyon which forms the frontier with north-eastern Argentina. To the west of the Paraná Plateau the land descends in foothills of red sandy soil to the Río Paraguay, which is a line of demarcation separating the undulating and densely-wooded eastern region from the grassy and scrub-covered plains of the Chaco. Two-thirds of the republic[1] lies to the west of the Río Paraguay. This western region is composed of unconsolidated, stoneless sands and clays brought from the Andes by the great rivers. It is drained by many small streams and by the Río Pilcomayo, which forms Paraguay's frontier with northern Argentina.

The contrast between these two areas—the wooded plateau on the one hand, and the Chaco plains on the other—is acute. Nowhere else in the world, perhaps, does a river divide so abruptly two such different lands. Eastern Paraguay, as J. Natalicio González states, is one of the best-watered areas in the world; but the west lacks running water. The east is all hills and meadows and forests; the west is a brackish prairie. The eastern forests are luxuriant, 'decorated like a woman with the grace of the orchid'; the vegetation is dense, giving shelter from the tempest and the summer sun; the sound of running water and the song of birds fill the air; there is an impression of harmony and of communal life. The western plains, however, are covered partly with dry grass and partly with trees that have few leaves and whose wood is as hard as steel. These trees in the west do not grow closely together but stand apart from one another, like palms, and they provide no shade from the sun, which scorches the earth. There is no sound of water or of birds. It is a lonely region, 'a plain with the soul of a mountain', motionless and hard as a rock.[2] The Paraguayans, however, consider that these two opposed regions are complementary to one another, and that together they form a natural unity. Natalicio González has written: 'Either of these two zones, taken separately, gives the impression of being somewhat fragmentary, incomplete, mutilated. From

---

[1] The total extent of Paraguay is approximately 157,047 sq. miles, the areas of the neighbouring countries being: Bolivia, 416,040; Brazil, 3,286,170; and Argentina, 1,079,965 sq. miles.

[2] J. Natalicio González, *Proceso y Formación de la Cultura Paraguaya* (Asunción and Buenos Aires, Guarania, 1938), pp. 17–20.

the synthesis of their opposites there arises a complex unity, peculiar in itself, the product of the marriage of contradictory telluric elements.'[1]

One-third of Paraguay is a natural Arcadia; but it takes more than a fertile soil and a healthy climate[2] to create a human Paradise. The story of Paraguay is one of wars and revolutions and, consequently, poverty—a sequence partly to be accounted for by the country's geographical situation. During the colonial period the inhabitants, distant and isolated in the centre of the south American mainland, were virtually 'an army on campaign':[3] they were constantly subject to attacks by the surrounding Indian tribes and, latterly, by the Mamelucos of southern Brazil; and, because they were an outpost established so far from the coasts and ports of the continent, they received a minimum of assistance from Spain in the developing of the land's natural resources. When the independent Republic came into being at the beginning of the nineteenth century, the remoteness of the new nation helped more than one local autocrat to erect an 'iron curtain' around it so that its people might be more thoroughly dominated. The geographical situation, too, has continued to have an unfortunate effect in later times; embedded between the hinterlands of two powerful and rival States, Argentina and Brazil, and blocking land-locked Bolivia's access to the great waterways that lead to the Atlantic Ocean, Paraguay has been involved in long and devastating wars with those three neighbours and is still the victim of political and economic pressure from, in particular, Argentina. Ascunción, the capital, situated on the eastern side of the Río Paraguay, is about 1,000 miles by river from the Atlantic, and the river route is still—and will long remain—the republic's lifeline; but 800 miles of the journey downstream are through foreign territory, and even in the first 200 miles—from Asunción to the junction of the Río Paraguay with the Río Paraná—the right

---

[1] ibid. p. 17.

[2] The Paraguayan climate is sub-tropical. Summer lasts from October to March, when the maximum temperature at Asunción is between 98° and 105° F. The mean temperature in the capital varies between 71° and 73° F. Asunción has an average annual rainfall of a little over 50 inches, the heaviest rains falling in December and March. Rainfall is highest on the Paraná plateau and diminishes towards the west. This shortage of rain in the Chaco, together with the porous nature of the alluvial soil, accounts for the dryness referred to by Natalicio González. The lowlands are often flooded, however, in the rainy season.

[3] Manuel Domínguez, *El Alma de la Raza* (Buenos Aires, Ayacucho, 1946), p. 23.

bank of the river is Argentine. The only railway connexion with the outer world is still by way of Argentina, and on the journey of 938 miles by rail to Buenos Aires no more than 274 miles of the track—from Asunción to Encarnación—are within the borders of Paraguay. At a moment's notice, therefore, the economy of Paraguay could be almost strangled by Argentina.

In these circumstances—remote, isolated, and liable to political, military, and economic pressure from all sides—it is perhaps not surprising that the Paraguayans should have fought so often. Nor is it to be wondered at that, in the enclosed world of Paraguay, political rivalries should have been bitter and dictatorships frequent. The only benefit that geographical remoteness and isolation have conferred on the people of this country is the creation and preservation of a racial homogeneity that is scarcely paralleled anywhere in Latin America.

Chapter II

GUARANÍES AND SPANIARDS

RACIAL ORIGINS

THE two distinctive regions in Paraguay have their counterpart in the twofold racial composition of the nation. The original inhabitants belonged to the linguistic family known as Tupí-Guaraní, and at present the population of about 2,000,000 is predominantly *mestizo*—i.e. they are descendants of the original Spanish colonists and women of Guaraní stock. The number of Spaniards who settled in Paraguay was relatively small, however, with the consequence that the Paraguayan *mestizo* has a much higher proportion of Indian blood than most others in Latin America.

The Tupí-Guaraní Indians probably originated in the Río Paraguay basin, and their centre was in the neighbourhood of the present site of Asunción. Thence they spread over a vast area of eastern South America between the Plata estuary and the northern Río Orinoco. Before the arrival of the Spaniards they practised a shifting cultivation of maize and mandioca (cassava), supplementing their diet with fish and game. Unlike the Indians of Argentina and Chile, they were in general a friendly race, though ferocious in battle.[1] They still retain those qualities today.

The Guaraníes were a people of the forest: their word for Paradise was Yvaga, which means 'a place of abundant fruit-trees',[2] and their language, which was largely onomatopœic in origin,[3] still preserves the sounds of the forest. They devised a mythology which enabled them to live in harmony with the prolific plant and animal life around them. Their principal god, Tupang, was a pure and formless spirit animating and impregnating the whole universe. Tupang shone in the lightning, roared in the thunder, became liquid in the rain, blazed in the sun, murmured in the leaves of the forest. He was incapable of doing or thinking evil: all his manifestations were good and well-intentioned. He did not pun-

[1] Preston E. James, *Latin America* (New York, Odyssey Press, 1950), p. 266.
[2] González, *La Cultura Paraguaya*, p. 25.
[3] In modern Guaraní, a machine-gun is *piripipí*, and the fire of a heavy machine-gun is *pororó*.

ish, or humiliate. He simply poured forth goodness everywhere. His actions proved that life on earth was not final, and the Guaraníes therefore had no great difficulty in amalgamating their own religion and Christianity when the Christian missionaries arrived to convert them in the sixteenth century.[1] The Guaraníes had no idols or temples, nor did they practise sacrificial rites. Of their numerous gods, only one was malevolent: all the others were protectors of trees and animals, dispensers of fertility and justice. Countless legends relating to the Guaraní gods and the creation of the indigenous trees and plants of Paraguay have been passed down orally and are repeated today in many different versions.

León Cadogan offers several possible interpretations of the word 'Paraguay'. The most probable origin of the country's name, he suggests, is that given by Ruiz de Montoya in his seventeenth-century *Tesoro de la Lengua Guaraní*. According to this writer, *para* in old Guaraní meant 'variety' and the verb *gua* was 'to adorn' or 'to crown'.[2] Thus 'Paraguay' would be a river that is variously crowned. At flood-time the Río Paraguay is crowned with floating islands, named *camalotes*, which are adorned with many-coloured water hyacinths. A whole series of legends has arisen in connexion with these *camalotes*, which are still a common feature of the Paraguayan river scene today. When the periodical floods occur, fragments of the banks are torn away by the torrent and float downstream bearing whatever vegetation may have been growing upon them. Sir Woodbine Parish, the first British chargé d'affaires at Buenos Aires, wrote that at flood time

it frequently happens that animals, to save themselves, swim off to the floating masses of canes and brushwood (called by the Spaniards 'camalotes'), and are thus carried down the river, and landed in the vicinity of the towns and villages upon the coast. Many strange stories are told of the unexpected visits of tigers so conveyed from their ordinary haunts to Buenos Ayres and Monte Video. One in my time was shot in my own grounds near Buenos Ayres, and some years before no less than four were landed in one night at Monte Video, to the great alarm of the inhabitants when they found them prowling about the streets in the morning.[3]

During Paraguay's war against the Triple Alliance of Brazil, Argentina, and Uruguay (1865–70) Marshal López sent raiding

[1] González, *La Cultura Paraguaya*, pp. 79–80.
[2] When used as a suffix, *gua* meant 'proceeding from'. G. Pendle, *Uruguay* (London, RIIA, 1952), p. 1.
[3] Sir Woodbine Parish, *Buenos Ayres and the Provinces of the Río de la Plata* (London, Murray, 1839), p. 187.

parties in canoes downstream to attack the Brazilian fleet on the river. These canoes were disguised with foliage to resemble *cama-lotes*.

Guaraní culture developed in the luxuriant eastern region be-tween the rivers Paraná and Paraguay; but a century or so before the coming of the Spaniards Guaraní warriors crossed the Río Paraguay, fought the local tribes and, after much bloodshed, temporarily succeeded in subduing them. This was the first of many Chaco wars. Natalicio González writes:

> Thereafter this feat would be constantly repeated in the course of our history. The occasion and the outward form have differed, according to the conditions of the epoch; but the act is always the same.[1]

After their success in the Chaco at some time in the fifteenth century, the Guaraníes proceeded towards the Inca empire in the Andes and thus came into contact with a civilization which was quite different from their own and whose basic materials were metals—gold, silver, and copper—instead of wood, stone, bones, and clay. Therefore when a few decades later the Spaniards, seek-ing a short cut to the mines of Peru, travelled up the great rivers to Paraguay, the Guaraníes whom they found there understood and sympathized with their purpose; and it so happened that these friendly Indians were the tribe most suited to collaborate in the enterprise of colonial development.

THE COMING OF THE SPANIARDS

The first white men to enter Paraguay were the Portuguese ad-venturer Aleixo Garcia and three or four companions, all of whom had crossed the South Atlantic with the Spanish navigator Díaz de Solís. These Europeans arrived at the Río Paraguay in 1524 and, having made an alliance with the Guaraníes, set out through the Chaco accompanied by some 2,000 Guaraní warriors. They reached the western fringes of the Inca territory, where they en-gaged in plunder. On their return to Paraguay, Garcia and his European colleagues were killed (the motive for the act is un-known) by their allies; but the news of the silver which they had brought back from the mountains was carried to the Spanish ex-plorers on the Atlantic coast and attracted Sebastián Cabot to the Río Paraguay for a short time in 1526. A few years later the Emperor Charles V was persuaded that the Portuguese had de-

---

[1] González, *La Cultura Paraguaya*, p. 90.

signs on Paraguay and the Plata basin; so in 1535 he dispatched
Pedro de Mendoza to the Río de la Plata, with instructions to
build forts, open the route to Peru, and colonize. Mendoza landed on the site of modern Buenos Aires—at that time a barren
region frequented by hostile Indians—and from that precarious
base he sent Juan de Ayolas upstream in search of El Dorado.
Ayolas travelled up the Río Paraná and some distance up the Río
Paraguay, whence he travelled into the Chaco, leaving Domingo
Martínez de Irala in charge of his boats on the river. When, in
August 1537, these boats needed repair they were taken into a
small bay on the eastern bank of the Paraguay, and a stockade
was erected there on a headland overlooking the water. Irala
seems to have been absent when the little fort on the riverside was
baptized Nuestra Señora de la Asunción, and it is generally accepted that the founder of the Paraguayan capital was another
member of Mendoza's company, Juan de Salazar y Espinosa.

In the following month—September 1537—Mendoza having
died on his way from Buenos Aires and Ayolas having failed to
return (he never did return) from his Chaco expedition, Martínez
de Irala was appointed governor of all the vast area claimed by
Spain in southern South America, with Asunción as headquarters.
The settlement at Buenos Aires lacked provisions and was constantly attacked by the pampa Indians: it was therefore evacuat-
ed in 1541, the colonists travelling upstream to join their compatriots at Asunción, where conditions were much more favour-
able.[1] The Guaraníes, a naturally friendly race, had special reasons for being co-operative: they wished to enlist the help of the
Spaniards in fighting against the enemy tribes who surrounded
them and, secondly, in resuming their endeavour to seize the
mineral wealth of Bolivia and Peru. Moreover, the land around
Asunción, in contrast to the pampa plains, was fabulously productive. Here the Spaniards to their delight found an abundance
of chickens, partridges, doves and ducks, mandioca, sweet pota-
toes, peanuts, maize, beans and pumpkins, deer, boars, river fish,
and a wonderful variety of fruits.[2] In addition Paraguay was
situated in a strategic position at the head of the great river system
which converged downwards from the El Dorado of the Andes to
the Atlantic Ocean and the maritime route to Europe.

[1] Buenos Aires was re-established by a governor of Paraguay, Juan de Garay,
in 1580.
[2] González, *La Cultura Paraguaya*, p. 97.

Very soon the Guaraníes swamped the Spaniards racially, and Paraguay became essentially a *mestizo* colony. The Guaraní women willingly bore children to the white men, and Governor Irala, for example, himself had several local concubines, as his last will and testament proves:

> Item. I say and declare and confess that I have and God has given me in this province certain daughters and sons, who are: Diego Martínez de Yrala and Antonio de Yrala and Doña Ginebra de Yrala, children of myself and María my servant . . .; and Doña Ysabel de Yrala, daughter of Agueda my servant; and Doña Ursula de Yrala, daughter of Leonor my servant; and Martín Pérez de Yrala, son of Scolástica my servant; and Ana de Yrala, daughter of Marina my servant; and María, daughter of Beatriz, servant of Diego de Villalpando.[1]

Four of Irala's daughters married captains. By encouraging miscegenation he earned for himself the title of 'Father of the Nation'.

THE JESUIT MISSIONS

Meanwhile, of course, the Catholic Church was at work side by side with the temporal authorities. The first bishop reached Asunción in 1556, and three Jesuits arrived in 1588 with the purpose of converting and subduing the Indians. The Jesuits operated principally in the south-eastern area of the country and on the eastern and southern bank of the Río Paraná in districts that are now incorporated in Brazil and Argentina. They gathered hundreds of Guaraní families into their mission towns, known as reductions, of which about thirty—with a total population of at least 100,000—were in existence by the end of the seventeenth century, eight of these towns being within the boundaries of modern Paraguay, where the ruins of the churches and houses can still be seen. Each town was built round a large central square which was covered with fine grass, kept short by pasturing sheep. One side of the square was formed by a towered church of stone or Paraguayan hardwood, and storehouses. The other three sides consisted of very long buildings, made of sun-dried bricks or wattled canes, in which the Indians lived. Each of these buildings accommodated 100 or more families in separate apartments, but all under one roof and veranda. The Guaraníes were indolent by nature and unaccustomed to systematic work, so the Jesuits organized their communities in a semi-communal manner. They

---

[1] Quoted by H. G. Warren, *Paraguay* (University of Oklahoma Press, 1949), pp. 79–80; González, *La Cultura Paraguaya*, pp. 207–10.

marshalled their neophytes to the sound of music, and in procession to the fields, with a saint borne high aloft, the community each day at sunrise took its way. Along the paths, at stated intervals, were shrines of saints, and before each of them they prayed, and between each shrine sang hymns. As the procession advanced, it became gradually smaller as groups of Indians dropped off to work the various fields, and finally the priest and acolyte with the musicians returned alone. At mid-day, before eating, they all united and sang hymns, and then, after their meal and siesta, returned to work till sundown, when the procession again reformed, and the labourers, singing, returned to their abodes.[1]

Other converts worked on the enormous *estancias* attending to the cattle that the Spaniards had introduced into the country and which had increased into many large herds. The Guaraníes were also taught to weave cotton, and they had tanneries, carpenters' shops, tailors, hat-makers, coopers, cordage-makers, boat-builders, cartwrights, and joiners. They made arms and powder and musical instruments, and produced beautiful manuscripts and printed books. All the lands and equipment were the property of the community, which worked under the direction of the two or three Jesuits who lived in each town. In exchange for their produce, the Indians received rations of food and clothing and of imported articles such as knives, scissors, and looking-glasses.[2] The main exports were *yerba mate*, cotton, tobacco, hides, and wood. The Jesuit reductions also served as a defensive line, and their armies protected Paraguay from the Portuguese Mamelucos who constantly raided the Spanish-owned territory from the region that is now southern Brazil.

Although Jesuit rule was in so many respects enlightened, it had its unfavourable aspect, as C. R. Boxer has explained:

The Jesuit attitude towards their charges was indeed a paternal one, but it was the attitude of a father towards a backward boy who is never expected to grow up. Their neophytes were never trained to look after themselves, but to follow blindly in all things the orders and advice of their spiritual fathers. When they had become men, they had no chance of putting away childish things. They were thus inherently incapable of taking their place in the civilized society which was slowly developing around them.[3]

---

[1] R. B. Cunninghame Graham, *A Vanished Arcadia* (London, Heinemann, 1901), pp. 178–9.

[2] ibid. pp. 180–2.

[3] C. R. Boxer, *Salvador de Sá and the Struggle for Brazil and Angola*, 1602–86 (University of London, Athlone Press, 1952), p. 127. Concerning the Jesuit reductions see also C. Lugon, *La République Communiste Chrétienne des Guaranis, 1610–1768*. Paris, Editions Ouvrières Economie et Humanisme, 1949.

It was inevitable that the wealth and power of the Jesuit 'empire within an empire' should arouse jealousy among the Spanish landowners in Paraguay who were eager to cut in on the Jesuits' profitable trade in *yerba mate* and obtain cheap Indian labour for their own enrichment. The Jesuits opposed the exploitation of the Indians: although they were strict in supervising the lives of their converts they themselves used no force except 'the Sword of the Word' and, in cases of misbehaviour, certain forms of punishment, including imprisonment. Local Spaniards were exasperated by this humane treatment of potential serfs and when slave-raiders from Brazil attacked the reductions the Spanish colonists made no serious efforts to help defend them. 'Being very anxious to secure the Guaraní Indians for forced labour on their own *encomiendas*, they preferred to dispute their possession with the Paulistas (i.e. the raiders from Sao Paulo), after the Reductions had been destroyed, rather than to see their potential labour-supply guarded from them by the Jesuits.'[1]

Complaints against the Jesuits and reports of their power caused increasing anxiety in Madrid, and in 1767 a royal decree was finally issued banishing all Jesuits from the Spanish dominions and ordering the seizure of their property. The clergy and civil administrators who were then sent from Buenos Aires to take charge of the missions were guilty of thorough mismanagement, and the Indians soon deserted the reductions and either returned to their old way of life or became peons on the large estates. Within a few years the Jesuit buildings were in ruins and overgrown by tropical vegetation; the herds had been reduced to a fraction of their former dimensions; and the orchards and fields were again jungle.

Although they were in the country for nearly 200 years, the Jesuits exercised little or no permanent influence on the development of the Paraguayan people and character. Their purpose was merely to 'domesticate' the Indians, not to develop Paraguayan civilization. Moreover, the Jesuits were celibates, and Paraguay was destined to be *mestizo*. The Guaraníes could not absorb them into their own race, so the Jesuits left almost no trace of their long residence—except the ruins of their villages, some of which, the vegetation having been removed from them, are now visible to the few tourists who visit the mission territory. The Spanish colonists, for their part, introduced many features of European

[1] ibid. p. 72.

civilization. Nevertheless, even today family life and popular be-
liefs are in many respects in the Guaraní tradition, and the melodious Guaraní language is still the language of the mass of the
population. Most people—and everyone in the towns—also
speak Spanish (although with a clearly perceptible Guaraní in-
tonation), but it is scarcely an exaggeration to say that 'almost all
conversations, beginning in Spanish, end in Guaraní.'[1] Indeed,
this language has become a symbol of national independence, and
in the Chaco War against Bolivia it was used as a secret code
which the Bolivians were unable to understand. Manuel Domínguez believed that the astuteness of the Paraguayans could be
partly explained by their constant mental exercise of speaking
two such very different languages.[2] Paraguay is the only truly
bilingual country in South America, and the only country in
which periodicals, plays, and poems are published in the indigenous language.[3]

[1] Jean Sermet, 'Le Paraguay', *Les Cahiers d'Outre-Mer*, vol. 3, no. 9 (Bordeaux,
Institut de la France d'Outre-Mer, 1950), p. 46.
[2] Domínguez, *El Alma de la Raza*, p. 29.
[3] For further references to Paraguayan bilingualism see below, pp. 56 and
81–2.

Chapter III

THE STRUGGLE FOR INDEPENDENCE

WHILE the Jesuits were organizing and expanding their missions in the Paraná region, the affairs of Paraguay proper continued to be directed by the Spanish authorities at Asunción, where rivalries among the leading citizens and Spain's representatives became endemic after 1544, the year in which the Governor of the time, Álvar Núñez Cabeza de Vaca, was deposed in a movement which has been described as Paraguay's first revolution.[1] Many of the officials appointed by metropolitan Spain were men of outstanding ability: conspicuous among them were Juan de Garay, who recognized that Paraguay needed a seaport and therefore sailed downstream to re-found Buenos Aires in 1580, and the locally-born Hernando Arias de Saavedra (known as Hernandarias), who governed the province with great foresight at the end of the sixteenth century and again at the beginning of the seventeenth. In this early period, thanks to the wisdom and initiative of Paraguay's governors, and because Asunción was still considered as a strategic town situated on a prospective short-cut to the mineral wealth of the Andes, a serious attempt was made to develop the colony by such measures as the importation of livestock and European seeds and the encouragement of skilled crafts: for example, carpentry and ship-building, in which local workmen became most proficient. But by 1617—when Spain decreed the separation of Asunción's offspring, Buenos Aires, from Paraguay—it had become apparent that the proposed route across the Chaco to the Andean mines was impracticable, and from that date Madrid's interest in Asunción declined. Buenos Aires increased in importance, and Paraguay now was no more than, firstly, a defensive outpost whose function was to hold back the Portuguese forces constantly pressing southwards from Brazil, and, secondly, a moderate source of revenue. It was natural that this state of affairs should cause dissatisfaction. Allegiance to the Spanish Crown was not questioned; but the Paraguayans increasingly resented the taxation and restrictions which Madrid

[1] W. H. Koebel, *Paraguay* (London, Fisher Unwin, 1919), p. 76.

13

imposed upon their commerce, and the fact that the Jesuits still had official support in their humane and profitable exploitation of the eastern area of the country.

So great was [Asunción's] distance from the mother country that the dreaded might of Spain, by the time that it had filtered across the ocean, along the coast, and up the great river system far inland, had lost much of its terror. The community which comprised the early white population of Paraguay was essentially of a daredevil order, otherwise it had never penetrated to that remote spot.[1]

The Guaraníes, moreover, with whom the Spaniards mixed, were a virile race. It is not surprising, therefore, that Paraguay should have been the scene of one of the earliest and most serious risings against Spanish authority to occur anywhere in the Spanish-American Empire; though it is an exaggeration to claim (as some Paraguayans have done) that this movement contained 'the spiritual elements which characterized the Spanish-American War of Independence which broke out almost ninety years later.'[2] Nevertheless, the rebellion which broke out in Paraguay during the 1720's had a nationalist flavour.

The origin of the prolonged insurrection was in 1721, when an ambitious visiting official, José Antequera y Castro, on his own initiative, successfully appealed to the leading citizens of Asunción to support him in overthrowing the Spanish Governor. Thereupon the Viceroy of Peru, in whose jurisdiction Paraguay now lay, tried to reinstate the deposed Governor. Turmoil followed: Antequera fled and was subsequently captured by the Spaniards and executed; but for nearly fifteen years the Paraguayan rebels, who named themselves *Comuneros* (i.e. 'of the people'), defied the King of Spain's representatives, and it was only when loyal troops defeated them in battle in 1735 that law and order were—though, even then, incompletely—restored. During this long period of *Comunero* unrest, neighbouring Indian tribes ravaged many districts of Paraguay, reaching indeed the gates of Asunción itself,[3] and the Portuguese, taking advantage of the disorder, completed their annexation of a large area in the north, which, ever since, has formed part of Brazil.

By 1776, in which year Paraguay was incorporated in the Viceroyalty of the Río de la Plata, the country had been impoverished

---

[1] Koebel, *Paraguay*, p. 25.   [2] ibid. p. 156.
[3] Warren, *Paraguay* (University of Oklahoma Press, 1949), p. 122.

by the cost of maintaining a permanent defensive system against aggression from outside, the meagreness of the income received in exchange for its valuable exports of *yerba* and other produce, and decades of neglect. To the prevalent discontent was now added resentment that in future Paraguay, as a member of the Viceroyalty of La Plata, was expected to take its orders from Buenos Aires; and when the *criollos* of that town declared, in effect, their independence from Spain in 1810 and called upon Asunción to do the same, the Paraguayans refused to do so. The Argentines therefore sent General Belgrano to force them to comply; but the courage of the Paraguayans had been underestimated; Belgrano's expedition was decisively defeated; and he withdrew from Paraguayan territory, leaving the local people more than ever determined to resist foreign interference. This determination became apparent two months later, when Paraguay's sixtieth and last Governor, a brigadier of the Spanish royal armies, decided to call in Portuguese forces to defend the province against any further attacks from Argentina. The Governor's proposal provoked an uprising at Asunción on 14 May 1811 and, immediately afterwards, his own deposition.

DR FRANCIA

Paraguay was now an independent State, and a man of iron will, Dr José Gaspar Rodríguez de Francia, was about to obtain absolute power over it. The Scottish merchant John Parish Robertson, who entered the country in 1811 or 1812, wrote (in later years) a vivid description of the future dictator as he was at the time of his arrival:

On one of those lovely evenings in Paraguay, after the south-west wind has both cleared and cooled the air, I was drawn, in my pursuit of game, into a peaceful valley. . . Suddenly I came upon a neat and unpretending cottage. Up rose a partridge; I fired, and the bird came to the ground. A voice from behind called out, 'Buen tiro'—'a good shot'. I turned round, and beheld a gentleman of about fifty years of age, dressed in a suit of black, with a large scarlet capote, or cloak, thrown over his shoulders. He had a maté-cup in one hand, a cigar in the other; and a little urchin of a negro, with his arms crossed, was in attendance by the gentleman's side. The stranger's countenance was dark, and his black eyes were very penetrating, while his jet hair, combed back from a bold forehead, and hanging in natural ringlets over his shoulders, gave him a dignified and striking air. He wore on his shoes large golden buckles, and at the knees of his breeches the same. . . In exercise of the primitive and

15

simple hospitality common in the country, I was invited to sit down under the corridor, and to take a cigar and maté. A celestial globe, a large telescope, and a theodolite were under the little portico; and I immediately inferred that the personage before me was no other than Doctor Francia... He introduced me to his library, in a confined room, with a very small window, and that so shaded by the roof of the corridor, as to admit the least portion of light necessary for study. The library was arranged on three rows of shelves, extending across the room, and might have consisted of three hundred volumes. There were many ponderous books on law; a few on the inductive sciences; some in French and some in Latin upon subjects of general literature, with Euclid's Elements, and some school-boy treatises on algebra. On a large table were heaps of law-papers and processes. Several folios bound in vellum were outspread upon it; a lighted candle (though placed there solely with a view to light cigars) lent its feeble aid to illumine the room; while a maté-cup and inkstand, both of silver, stood on another part of the table. There was neither carpet nor mat on the brick-floor; and the chairs were of such ancient fashion, size, and weight, that it required a considerable effort to move them from one spot to another. They were covered with old tanned ox-leather, indented with curious hieroglyphics, and, from long use, very brown and glossy. Their straight backs were conspicuously higher than the head of the party seated upon them, and to sit in a reclining position was out of the question. The ground of the apartment was scattered over with thousands of pieces of torn letters, and untorn envelopes. An earthen jar for water and a jug stood upon a coarse wooden tripod in one corner, and the Doctor's horse-furniture in another. Slippers, boots, and shoes lay scattered about, and the room altogether had an air of confusion, darkness, and absence of comfort, the more striking that the cottage, though lowly, was perfectly neat outside, and so romantically placed, as to have all the air of an abode at once of beauty and of peace...

He made some display of his acquaintance with Voltaire, Rousseau, and Volney, and he concurred entirely in the theory of the latter. But he was most of all proud to be known as an algebraist and astronomer... In Paraguay, an acquaintance with French, Euclid's Elements, equations, the mode of handling a theodolite, or with books prohibited by the Vatican, was, in point of knowledge, so much the exception to the general rule, that the man who had it ... was deemed something between a magician and a demi-god.[1]

Francia had studied theology and law at the College of Monserrat in the University of Córdoba, in what is now Argentina. His literary attainments and his possession of the instruments of science were sufficient to make him feared by the simple Para-

[1] J. P. and W. P. Robertson, *Letters on Paraguay*, vol. 1, pp. 330–6.

guayans, who already looked upon him as a magician before he became head of the State. In 1814 a motley Congress which he had summoned to meet in Asunción voted him absolute power for three years. Two years later he was appointed dictator for life, with the title of *El Supremo*, and he did in fact maintain his hold upon the country until his death in 1840. During this long period he governed by means of the army and a host of spies, and the number of his summary punishments and executions cannot be estimated. His enemies exaggerated the cruelties committed, but it is true that Francia dealt ruthlessly with persons whom he suspected of plotting against the régime or of intriguing on behalf of Buenos Aires, and, indeed, anyone who tried to thwart him. At this time Spain's restrictions on trade and immigration having been removed, European pioneers and speculators were pouring into the liberated territories of Latin America; but Francia, fearing that foreigners who might enter Paraguay would exploit the country and undermine his own position, soon stopped all personal and commercial intercourse with the outside world. Foreigners who had already reached Asunción—among them John Parish Robertson and his brother—were expelled and forbidden to return. Emigration was prohibited, the Church victimized, and education neglected. Nevertheless, even the bitterest enemies of Dr Francia conceded that he was a man of complete honesty, utterly incorruptible, disinterested, frugal and tirelessly hardworking, and that he genuinely loved the nation even while he oppressed it. His dictatorship was stern and brutal; but at least Paraguay during this period was spared the anarchy which prevailed in most of the other countries newly emancipated from Spain. The *Supremo's* isolationist policy ruined Paraguay's external trade; but it compelled the Paraguayans to develop and diversify their internal economy; it increased their national consciousness and self-reliance; and, by preventing the influx of aliens it preserved the homogeneity of the people. When Francia died, Paraguay was more isolated, but also more stubbornly independent, than ever before. Dreaded in his lifetime, *El Supremo*—not without justification—is revered today as one of the great national heroes.[1]

---

[1] Strangely enough, it was in England that his rehabilitation began, and as early as 1843, the year in which Thomas Carlyle published his essay *Dr Francia*, wherein the hero-worshipper expressed doubts on the accuracy of Parish Robertson's portrait of the dictator as an unmitigated villain.

Paraguay

CARLOS ANTONIO LÓPEZ

The death of Francia was followed by a few months of uncertainty and disorder. Then a Congress was called, the embargo on foreign trade was lifted, and it became apparent that the destinies of Paraguay were now to be dominated by an able man of mixed *criollo* and *mestizo* blood: Carlos Antonio López. A republican Constitution was drawn up, and López was nominated the country's all-powerful first President. Meanwhile, however, the dictator Rosas at Buenos Aires forced Paraguay into a further period of isolation by closing the Río de la Plata to Paraguayan shipping, and this ban continued in force until Rosas's fall in 1852, in which year an English scientist C. B. Mansfield visited Ascunción. Mansfield wrote of López:

I have only seen the President once since I was introduced to him. I then met him on the road as I was out riding; he was coming into town from his country-house in a queer old coach—the only one in the place—with as great an escort of soldiers and officers as the Queen would have. Everybody is obliged to stop and take off their hats when he passes; so of course I did so, and received a most gracious bow in return. In Francia's time everybody was forced to take off their hats to every soldier, and the country-boys, who wear no clothes at all, were obliged to wear hats for the purpose of saluting them. . . The President himself rarely sees or receives any society: he is, I suppose, more utterly alone than any man in the world, for, unlike other kings, he has neither ministers nor advisers of any kind; everything is arranged by his own head, every officer of the executive appointed by him. The Bishop is his brother too, and the General of the army his son. The President is immensely fat: as he sat to receive me with his hat on, cocked a little on one side, he looked like George the Fourth.[1]

Although Paraguay now had a Constitution, Carlos Antonio López was just as absolute a ruler as Francia had been, and, unlike *El Supremo*, he amassed a huge fortune during his presidency. He became the country's principal landowner, acquired enormous herds of cattle, and the trade in *yerba*, which was now a government monopoly, of itself provided him with a princely income. Nevertheless, López was a relatively enlightened despot, and, especially after the overthrow of Rosas and the reopening of Paraguay's river communications in 1852, he did his utmost to obtain foreign assistance in improving the economy of the Repub-

[1] C. B. Mansfield, *Paraguay, Brazil, and the Plate* (Cambridge, Macmillan, 1856), pp. 386–8.

lic. López made roads; employed a British firm to begin, in 1858, the construction of one of the first railways in South America; built a cathedral; expanded primary education; sent young Paraguayans to Europe to study and his son, Francisco Solano, to buy European armaments; and invited foreign surgeons, engineers, and mechanics to settle in Paraguay. In the early years of his rule López was greatly influenced by the North American 'arch-promoter' Edward A. Hopkins,[1] who was active in the development of such enterprises as river shipping, brick-making, and the timber and tobacco industries; but by 1854 Hopkins was out of favour and the most helpful foreigners in the main were British. A Dr Stewart and some colleagues, who had been army surgeons in the Crimean War, were given military rank in Paraguay and organized a hospital service. A certain Whitehead constructed an arsenal at Asunción, employing

300 natives and 30 English artisans in the work. The machinery was very complete, including besides the iron foundry a steam saw-mill for cutting the hard woods of the country. In three years the arsenal turned out 7 fine steamers, which plied as mail-boats from Asunción to Montevideo, and were afterwards armed as war-steamers. Heavy artillery (68-pounders) were also cast, for the batteries of Humaitá.[2]

George Thompson, a railway engineer, 'soon became one of the best Guaraní scholars in the country'[3] and later distinguished himself as an officer in the Paraguayan army. And there were many others who brought the techniques—and the manufactures—of Western civilization to this remote land which for so long had been inaccessible.

Carlos Antonio's gravest problem was the gradual deterioration in his relations with foreign States. In addition to a protracted but not very important quarrel with the United States, he was involved in a serious dispute with the Government at Buenos Aires, who refused to recognize Paraguay's independence, and with Brazil, concerning his northern frontier and the freedom of navigation on the Río Paraguay, which river was the only easy route to the Brazilian town of Corumbá in the land-locked territory of Mato Grosso. In these ominous conditions it was quite

---

[1] T. B. Jones, *South America Rediscovered* (University of Minnesota Press, 1949), p. 84; Warren, *Paraguay*, pp. 190–6.
[2] M. G. Mulhall, *The English in South America* (Buenos Aires, 'The Standard', 1878), p. 364.
[3] ibid. p. 365.

natural that President López should create, as he did, a powerful army. There is no doubt that at the time of his death in 1862 he was aware of the danger of war with Brazil. He was succeeded by his son, Francisco Solano, who inherited the international troubles.

SOLANO LÓPEZ AND THE WAR OF THE TRIPLE ALLIANCE

Francisco Solano López, born in 1826, was a brigadier-general at the age of eighteen, pandered to by his father, and treated (Cunninghame Graham suggests) as 'a little sultan' in the home.[1] At twenty-seven he travelled to Paris in luxury, returning to his native land with a handsome and ambitious Irish mistress, Mme Lynch, who remained beside him throughout his disastrous military campaigns, bore him a number of children, and, when he was finally cornered by the enemy and killed, buried him with her own hands in the red soil of Paraguay.[2] Solano López aroused such violent hatred and also received such extravagant adulation that it is difficult to form an accurate opinion of his character and career. None of the contemporary commentators and few, if any, of the many later writers on the subject can be accepted as completely unbiased. The engineer Thompson, who served López faithfully in the most dangerous and hopeless circumstances but who, at the end, described him as 'a monster without parallel',[3] wrote:

Francisco Solano López is a very stout man. . . He is short, but has a commanding presence. . . He is careful of his appearance, fond of military finery, especially in his staff, and has a somewhat peculiar strut when walking. His legs are short, with a decided bend backwards. He has a good seat on horseback, and when young used to be a hard rider. Now, however, it is a labour for him to get on and off his horse. He is of very indolent habits; will sit down for many hours, talking, or stand an equally long time, his walks limiting themselves to one or two hundred yards. He is extremely fond of Mrs. Lynch's children, but not of his other ones, of whom he has a number by different women. He entertains friendly feelings for no one, as he has shot almost all those who have been most favoured by himself, and who have been for years his only companions. He is a great smoker, and lover of the table; he eats enormously;

---

[1] Cunninghame Graham, *Portrait of a Dictator* (London, Heinemann, 1933), p. 91. This book, in which López is portrayed as a bloodthirsty tyrant, has been banned in Paraguay.

[2] C. A. Washburn, *The History of Paraguay* (Boston, Lee & Shepard, 1871), vol. 2, p. 594.

[3] George Thompson, *The War in Paraguay* (London, Longmans, 1869), p. v.

after dinner, when in a good humour, he occasionally sings a short song. . . Lopez speaks French fluently, always conversing in that language with Mrs. Lynch, who was educated in France. He knows a very little English, and of course Spanish well, that being the official language of the country; however, he never spoke anything but Guaraní to the men and officers, including myself. . . Lopez is a good speaker, especially in the kind of oratory likely to inspire his troops with confidence in himself and themselves, and with contempt for the enemy. . . He has an iron will, and an intense pride. . . He is, when he likes, very smooth and gentlemanly, and capable of imposing even on diplomats, and making them believe anything he wishes.[1]

When Solano López succeeded his father in 1862 chronic disorder still prevailed in Uruguay—a buffer State at the estuary of the Río de la Plata separating the great nations of Brazil and Argentina, and coveted by both. López, probably encouraged by Mme Lynch, was determined not only that Paraguay should be recognized as possessing equal rights with the larger Powers of South America, but also that his country should play an important role among the nations of the Plata region; and he quite rightly looked upon the interference of Brazil in the internal affairs of Uruguay as an obstacle to the fulfilment of his plans. By 1864, the Brazilians having meanwhile resorted to armed intervention in Uruguay (whose interests in the game of power politics were identical with those of Paraguay), López decided to take the initiative: he seized a valuable Brazilian ship on the Río Paraguay and sent an expedition to plunder the upstream Brazilian region of Mato Grosso. He then committed a fatal error. Instead of wooing Brazil's natural rival, Argentina, he sent an army across Argentine territory in a desperate and unsuccessful attempt to conquer southern Brazil and thereby secure the evacuation of Uruguay. The immediate result of this campaign was the formation in 1865 of a formidable anti-Paraguayan alliance: Brazil and its satellite, Uruguay, were joined by Argentina in a solemn pact to destroy Solano López. Once again Paraguay was enclosed behind an iron curtain.[2]

The odds against the Marshal (as López had himself named) were overwhelming; but he was at the head of a compact, homogeneous, and courageous nation; he held the interior lines and was fighting on his own soil; his enemies, moreover, were a

[1] ibid. pp. 326–7.
[2] The standard work on this period: P. H. Box, *The Origins of the Paraguayan War*, 2 vols. (Urbana, Illinois, 1929).

very mixed company, subject to internal rivalries, finding it difficult to work harmoniously together, and having to transport their
armies and supplies long distances up the Río Paraguay past forti-
fied positions and across the rapid waters of the Paraná. López
had rashly dissipated his original forces in the expeditions to
Mato Grosso and southern Brazil; but thereafter, when compelled
to wage an essentially defensive war, he displayed remarkable in-
genuity and, as was necessary in the circumstances, ruthless determination. Throughout the conflict he never forgave defeats
suffered by his troops; the officers were expected to observe liter-
ally the command 'conquer or die', and if they emerged alive
from defeat, the Marshal had them executed. Driven desperate by
disaster, and to diminish the chances of disintegration in his camp,
López decreed the torture and massacre of real or suspected trait-
ors and conspirators, while the women worked in the fields, made
clothes for the soldiers, and sometimes themselves took up arms to
fight beside the men. Cholera spread through the army and
among the people of Asunción. Garrisons—such as the heroic de-
fenders of the riverside fortress at Humaitá—suffered starvation.
Year after year the retreating Paraguayans resisted with incred-
ible tenacity, until finally in 1870 López was killed by a lance
thrust at Cerro Corá, and the war ended.

Paraguay was exhausted. In the peace settlement Brazil received the disputed territory in the north, as far as the Río Apá,
and Argentina's possession of the former Jesuit mission area east
of the Paraná was confirmed; but Paraguay's greatest loss was
that of its man-power during the five years of warfare. It is estimated that at the beginning of the conflict the population was
525,000 and that by 1871 it had been reduced to 221,079. Of
these survivors, 106,254 were women, 86,079 children, and only
28,746 men.[1]

Many panegyrics have been written about Marshal López, who
today is the greatest of all Paraguay's heroes. In a comparatively
moderate eulogy, Natalicio González says that 'a whole Race was
incarnate in him, a youthful, artistic and courageous Race, who
knew how to snatch from the claws of death the secret of Immor-
tality.'[2] The foreign reader normally dismisses laudatory flourishes
of that kind as rhetorical nonsense; but a perceptive Brazilian,

---

[1] Warren, *Paraguay*, p. 243.
[2] González, *Solano López y Otros Ensayos* (Paris, Editorial las Indias, 1926),
p. 3.

Walter Wey,[1] has argued that Paraguayan panegyrics must be considered in their historical context. The purpose of writers such as Juan O'Leary[2]—who, perhaps because of some Irish blood in his veins, greatly exceeds Natalicio González in exaggeration—has been to revive the faith and hope of a defeated race. For this reason many distinguished authors have not measured their words.

After the end of the so-called War of the Triple Alliance, Brazilian and Argentine forces occupied the defeated country for six years. Fortunately, however, the rivalry and suspicion prevailing between Rio de Janeiro and Buenos Aires favoured Paraguay's independence. Few educated Paraguayans had survived the war; the people had no political tradition except autocracy; and during the next half century Asunción suffered a succession of revolutions and coups d'état; between 1870 and 1932 Paraguay had one triumvirate and thirty-two Presidents. Partly because of this chronic disorder, attempts to stimulate immigration met with little success; but the failure of some of the colonization schemes was the fault of their foreign promoters, or of the colonists themselves. The most disastrous of these ventures was launched as early as 1872. A loan for Paraguay having been negotiated in London, a portion of it was set aside to finance a settlement of 'Lincolnshire Farmers' at a short distance from Asunción; but the contractors, instead of enrolling farmers in Lincolnshire, collected 800 'needy artisans from the streets of London' and sent them out to Paraguay, where no preparations had been made to house or feed them. For some months the colonists suffered severely from exposure and undernourishment. The survivors eventually received help from British residents in Argentina and were able to reach Buenos Aires, where most of them obtained employment. 'Only two families remained in Paraguay, and of the 800 colonists who had arrived from England in December 1872 no fewer than 162 died in the six months which intervened.'[3]

A more ambitious scheme, 'New Australia',[4] was launched in

---

[1] Walter Wey, *La Poesía Paraguaya*, tr. fr. Portuguese by H. Lagomarsino y Gladys Torres (Montevideo, Biblioteca Alfar, 1951), pp. 41–2.

[2] The attitude of Juan O'Leary is particularly remarkable because his mother was a victim of Solano López's persecution (Cunninghame Graham, *Portrait of a Dictator*, pp. 82–5, and p. 227).

[3] Mulhall, *The English in South America*, pp. 370–1.

[4] W. H. Koebel, *Paraguay* (London, Fisher Unwin, 1917), pp. 266–74 and H. V. Livermore, 'New Australia', *Hispanic American Historical Review*, August 1950, pp. 290–313.

1893 under the influence of the socialist theories of William Lane, an English-born journalist and teacher living in Queensland. In 1890 a general strike had been called by the Australian Labour Federation, who demanded the nationalization of all forms of property. The strike finally collapsed and was followed by an economic crisis and unemployment. In these circumstances Lane proposed that discontented workers should emigrate to South America and set up a co-operative Utopia of their own. He inspired the creation of the New Australia Co-operative Settlement Association, to which body the Paraguayan Government made a grant of about 450,000 acres of fertile land in the neighbourhood of Villarrica, and a prospectus was issued announcing that the object of the enterprise was 'to show the world that, under fair conditions, even workers can live a life worth living'. The settlers surrendered all their possessions to the common fund of the Association; they pledged themselves to teetotalism 'until the initial difficulties of settlement have passed'; and a first contingent of 250 emigrants embarked at Sydney in a small sailing-ship, the *Royal Tar*. Arrived at Villarrica, they set to work building adobe huts and fencing their pastures for cattle. Dissension soon developed, however, several of the colonists having broken their pledge of abstinence by drinking 'Paraguayan rum' (*caña*). These men were expelled from the colony by Lane, and were joined by a number of voluntary seceders. There were grievances and intrigues, and the women 'gave trouble', some husbands complaining that 'while perfectly contented with their day's work they were positively afraid to face the nocturnal music in their connubial tents.' In 1894 a second party of 225 arrived from Adelaide, and shortly afterwards Lane, unable to control the situation at Nueva Australia, moved some distance away to found the smaller colony at Cosmé. Subsequently the co-operative system was abandoned as unworkable. The remaining colonists acquired land of their own. Many of them prospered, and their descendants still live in the neighbourhood of Villarrica. León Cadogan, the anthropologist, is one of them.

The population of Paraguay grew until, by 1932, the losses sustained during the War of the Triple Alliance had been more than made up; but immigration contributed little to this increase. Immigrants during the period 1905–25 numbered no more than 13,258, most of them being Germans, Spaniards, and Italians.[1]

[1] Warren, *Paraguay*, p. 269.

Nevertheless, in the sixty years following the death of López, considerable progress was made in the social and economic reconstruction of Paraguay. A Constitution which was drawn up in 1870 did at least lay the foundation for party government, though it was ineffective in practice. Private foreign capital was enabled to assist in the development of the cattle, petit-grain,[1] and tannin industries, public utilities and general commerce. Banks were founded. The army was reorganized. Education was given a new start, and Paraguay experienced its 'golden age' in literature.

THE CHACO WAR

Social progress was destined to be interrupted by another long period of hostilities, the result, again, of Paraguay's geographical position.

While the Paraguayans were beginning to recover from their defeat by the Triple Alliance, Chile, far away on the western side of the continent, defeated the combined forces of Peru and Bolivia in the War of the Pacific (1879–83) and deprived the latter nation of its vitally important Pacific coastline. Bolivia thereby became a landlocked country, embittered, frustrated, and now desiring, as a substitute for its lost Pacific outlet, a passage by way of the Chaco and the Río Paraguay to the Atlantic. This reorientation of policy at La Paz was bound to lead to friction with Asunción, and, as the years passed, there were growing reasons for supposing that neither party would hesitate to use force. Bolivia and Paraguay had both met with military catastrophe in the second half of the nineteenth century, and the two countries were recuperating simultaneously; they were both building up new armies which would welcome an opportunity to wipe out the memory of previous disaster; both considered that they had a historical right to possession of the Chaco, and they had both established outposts (*fortines*) in that desolate region of floods and droughts in support of their claims, and, finally, the knowledge that oil deposits existed in the Chaco increased their determination to expel foreign intruders. When skirmishes between Paraguayan and Bolivian patrols were reported in 1928, nationalists on both sides found no difficulty in fomenting popular indignation.

War broke out officially in 1932 in spite of the efforts of other

---

[1] The small dried unripe fruit of the bitter orange from which oil of petit-grain was originally extracted. This oil is now obtained from the leaves and twigs of the tree. Used extensively in the perfume industry.

American countries and the League of Nations to prevent it. The Bolivians were confident of rapid victory. They greatly out-numbered the Paraguayans; their army had been trained under the supervision of a German general, Hans Kundt; and large quantities of surplus equipment from the First World War, in-cluding aeroplanes, had been imported from Great Britain and the United States. As so often before, however, the martial spirit and national solidarity of the Paraguayans were underestimated; the Paraguayans, again, had the interior lines and were near their base; and they were better acquainted than the Bolivians with the territory of the Chaco, where the Paraguayan hero, Colonel José Félix Estigarribia—who had the whole-hearted support of the able President of the Republic, Eusebio Ayala—brilliantly out-witted General Kundt. The Bolivian army consisted mostly of Indians, devoid of patriotism, who had been brought down from the Andean altitudes to fight in the remote and strange lowland jungle, 'green hell'. Large bodies of men could not operate effect-ively in this bewildering region. Special tactics had to be devised; and so Estigarribia, profiting by the wood-craft and self-reliance of his soldiers, sent them in small groups or singly behind the Bolivian lines to cut their communications and seize supplies. Casualties in the fighting and from disease were heavy on both sides; but the Paraguayans steadily advanced. In the end, how-ever, they were unable to invade the highlands of Bolivia and therefore could not secure a complete victory. In June 1935 both Governments agreed to an armistice, and peace negotiations—which were conducted with the aid of neutral Powers—continued until a treaty was finally signed in July 1938. By this settlement Paraguay gained possession of most of the extensive area of the Chaco that Estigarribia's troops had conquered during three years of painful and costly fighting.

Paraguayans look upon the Chaco War as a natural, necessary, and glorious phase in the development of their nationality. Justo Pastor Benítez has written:

The country needed a landmark to indicate the termination of decadence and to conclude the process of territorial demarcation; a victory, which would revive the faith that had been slumbering and which would waken the moral forces that lie in the depths of history.[1]

---

[1] Justo Pastor Benítez, *Estigarribia, el Soldado del Chaco* (Buenos Aires, Difusam, 1943), p. 27.

Chapter IV

WRITERS AND POLITICIANS, 1870–1935

As has been seen, after the death of Marshal López (1870) the process of national reconstruction was painful and protracted. Control of the State was in the hands of military officers and political opportunists with—as an intellectual class developed—the ever-increasing participation of men of letters. Indeed, until well after the end of the Chaco War (1935) Paraguayan historians, essayists, and poets almost without exception wrote on national themes and played an active part in day-by-day politics. Four intellectuals—Cecilio Báez, Manuel Gondra, Eligio Ayala, and Eusebio Ayala—became Presidents of the Republic (each of the last three held office for two terms); and many authors held diplomatic posts and portfolios in the Governments which succeeded one another with disturbing rapidity. Even today literature is inundated with patriotic eulogies and partisan denunciations, and there are few writers who avoid being involved in political controversy. The two contemporary authors quoted above—Natalicio González and Pastor Benítez—were Deputies in the national Congress and have held high office: González was for a short time President of the Republic, and Pastor Benítez has been a member of several Governments. Like so many other twentieth-century writers, they have both spent long periods in exile.

In general, therefore, the literature of Paraguay cannot be classified according to literary schools: it is a literature of individual writers, each of whom—with the exception of a few poets—must be considered in his political setting. The first notable figure is Juan Silvano Godoi, who was fifteen years of age when the War of the Triple Alliance officially began (1865). He spent the war years studying law in Argentina, where, as the news of his compatriots' heroic though hopeless martial feats reached him, he grew determined that Paraguay must again be strengthened. In 1870 this ardent, romantic, and violent man returned to Asunción to assist in the national recovery. He was prominent among those who drafted the somewhat idealistic Constitution of 1870, but was soon convinced that the Paraguayans had not yet outgrown the need for a more authoritarian form of government. This requirement was fulfilled, however, by a war hero, General Bernardino Caballero, who in 1874 founded a Conservative Party—the Colorados—and personally appointed the Governments of the country for the next thirty years. In 1877 Godoi, after the failure of a 'Liberal' revolution in which he had participated, had to flee abroad. In exile he became a successful business man, amassed a considerable fortune, and financed another abortive revolution in 1889. He then renewed his exile in Buenos Aires, again succeeded in commerce, abandoned politics, and dedicated himself once more to intellectual pursuits, writing books about the war. When he was at last allowed to return to Paraguay in 1895, Godoi brought with him his library and a valuable collection of paintings by European artists. With this material he created the Godoi Museum, which was later taken over by the State and is still in existence at Asunción. Before his death this gifted and intolerant man of letters served as Minister to Brazil.

The 'golden age' in Paraguayan literature was at its zenith about the year 1900, one of its most distinguished writers being Cecilio Báez, born in 1862, a lawyer by training and a teacher by vocation. In countless newspaper articles and lectures Báez preached nineteenth-century liberal ideas in this land of coups d'état and demagogism. Although Paraguay never became the democracy that he wished to make it, his pronouncements greatly influenced public opinion during his lifetime. Báez was largely responsible not only for the organization of the Liberal Party in 1887, but also for the overthrow of the long-established Colorado régime in 1904; he never ceased to demand more and better education; he advocated religious toleration (this policy made it necessary for him to attack the Catholic Church); and he recommended administrative decentralization. He occupied the highest posts in the State and in the University. In his democratic zeal, he wrote one of the bitterest condemnations of Marshal López. He published a number of books, among them: *Resumen de la Historia del Paraguay*, *Ensayo sobre el doctor Francia y la Dictadura en Sudamérica*, and *Historia Diplomática del Paraguay*. Like many other Paraguayan authors, he wrote polemically and carelessly, without caution or revision.

Báez's contemporary, Manuel Domínguez, was born at the village of Itauguá (where women for generations have worked fine and distinctive 'spider's web' lace, *ñandutí*) in 1867. He was a talented lyrical writer and a brilliant orator who had a tempestuous political career. His writing dealt with the usual topics: Paraguay's glorious past and the indomitable spirit of the people. His major literary achievement was a volume of essays entitled *El Alma de la Raza*. The style now seems rather affected. In politics, Domínguez began as a Deputy to Congress, and he was later Minister of Foreign Affairs and Vice-President of the Republic. He experienced a period of exile, delivered lectures on a wide range of subjects, was an expert on Paraguay's claims in the Chaco, and, when he died in 1935, was honoured both as the country's leading Bohemian and a fervent patriot.

The third of the outstanding figures of the literary-political 'generation of 1900' was Manuel Gondra, born in 1871 of a Paraguayan mother (whose nationality he adopted) and an Argentine father. Gondra was a literary critic, an educationalist, a diplomat, a minister in more than one Liberal Government, twice President of the Republic and, throughout his political career, a patriotic student of Paraguayan history, with special reference to frontier and Chaco problems. In his writing and in politics he was a man of impeccable integrity, modest, sincere, and respected by his countrymen; but he was born to teach rather than to command, and he was more impressive as an example than as a ruler. His periods as President (1910 and 1920) were brief, but entirely honourable, and although he suffered many changes of fortune, he always remained an imposing, reliable, and irrepressible person. Gondra, unlike the majority of Paraguayan authors, took infinite pains in revising everything that he wrote, and he was equally painstaking in his unsuccessful efforts to unite the four or five factions in the Liberal Party, whose disagreements for so long had complicated the Paraguayan political scene and contributed in so great a measure to the national instability.

Other talented members of the 1900 group of political men of letters were Fulgencio R. Moreno (born 1872, Deputy, Senator, Cabinet Minister, diplomat, authority on the Chaco boundaries, historical journalist), Juan E. O'Leary (born 1882, author of many books on the War of the Triple Alliance and Marshal López, whose reputation he defended with excessive passion and eloquence),[1] Arsenio López Decoud, Ignacio A. Pane, and the

[1] Moreno and O'Leary were technically Colorados, but they both on occasion collaborated with Liberal Governments.

two Ayalas. The least politically-minded writers of this remarkable generation were, perhaps, Alejandro Guanes (who wrote
lyrical poetry in classical form) and Eloy Fariña Núñez (a poet of
the Paraguayan countryside and of the Guaraníes, their legends
and folklore); but even these relatively 'pure' poets also contributed to political journalism.

Eligio Ayala, born in 1879, was active in the political disturb-
ances of the first decade of the twentieth century and then, after
returning to Asunción from a visit to Europe, was a prominent
figure in the Government and in diplomacy, and twice President.
A solitary and nervous man, quarrelsome and versatile, he wrote
prolifically on Paraguayan affairs, art, and literature. He reorganized the country's finances and administration, believed in
'private enterprise' in the economic sphere, and was a loyal and
incorruptible public servant.

Eusebio Ayala's second term as President coincided with the
Chaco War. He was born in 1874, and was a man of outstanding
intellect and far from handsome appearance.[1] He studied law,
read Darwin and the followers of Herbert Spencer, lectured,
wrote essays on education and history, became a successful banker,
travelled many times to Europe and also visited the United States.
He was acquainted with the German universities, attended lectures by Bergson, and subsequently specialized in political economy and international law. In speech and in writing he expressed
himself abruptly but clearly (an unusual technique in Latin
America), and he exerted a powerful civilizing influence upon
the Paraguayans of his time. Ayala, however, was a member of
the Liberal oligarchy, who, although they gave Paraguay a form
of democracy, were never a popular party. The Liberals were
liberal in their ideas, after the nineteenth-century fashion; but
they made little or no attempt to enter into contact with the less
privileged classes of society. Because the leading members of the
party had travelled widely and were known to have financial,
commercial, and social connexions abroad (in Argentina, Brazil,
Europe, and the United States), they were accused of serving
foreign interests; and because they failed to introduce drastic
social and economic reforms, they never won the sympathy of the
mass of the population. Eusebio Ayala was overthrown in a coup
d'état which occurred shortly after the end of the Chaco War, and

---

[1] Small of stature, Eusebio Ayala had 'a toucan nose' (Benítez, *El Solar Guaraní*, p. 155).

he died in exile in Buenos Aires six years later. By 1936 the liberal-minded 'generation of 1900' had fulfilled its function, and with Ayala's fall from power a new phase began in the evolution of Paraguay.

Chapter V

COLONEL FRANCO, ESTIGARRIBIA, AND MORÍNIGO

THE insurgents who in 1936 overthrew Eusebio Ayala, thereby ending a relatively long period of Liberal rule, came from different social groups. Policarpo Artaza, expressing the Liberal attitude to this so-called 'Liberating Revolution', states that its organizers were of three main classes: dissatisfied military officers (who, now that the fighting was over, feared that Estigarribia would retire them from the army, a process which had already begun), unsuccessful anti-Liberal politicians (who could not expect to attain power by democratic methods), and certain persons with ideological principles.[1] Discontent certainly existed after the end of the war. Many Paraguayans who had experienced comradeship and 'solidarity'[2] on the Chaco battlefields, felt that the old political parties and rivalries were stupid and out of date. Soldiers and civilians complained that the Liberals had shown undue leniency in the peace negotiations with defeated Bolivia. It was widely believed that the Liberal oligarchy was unfit to deal with Paraguay's current economic problems (which were aggravated by the world-wide depression of the 1930's) and that this prosperous group had no intention of introducing the social reforms which obviously were necessary. Too much land (nationalists and labour argued) was in the hands of foreign companies and of a few wealthy families; the standard of living of the working class in town and country was appallingly low; and the welfare services, education, and industry were quite inadequate for the needs of the time.

COLONEL FRANCO

As was to be expected, a number of young men (among them, many university students) were attracted by the totalitarian

---

[1] Policarpo Artaza, *Ayala, Estigarribia y el Partido Liberal* (Buenos Aires, Editorial Ayacucho, 1946), pp. 151–5. Artaza owned one of the country's leading newspapers, *El País*, which was seized by the insurgents. He went into exile.

[2] This is the word used by the principal apologist of the Liberating Revolution, Juan Stefanich. See in particular his *El Paraguay Nuevo* (Buenos Aires, Editorial Claridad, 1943), p. 57.

theories of government which were then gaining ground in Europe, and these aspiring politicians spoke eloquently of creating 'The New Paraguay'—a project which naturally appealed to the labour leaders, though the enthusiasts had not yet drawn up a detailed statement of their intentions. A popular hero of the Chaco War, Colonel Rafael Franco, came forward, with the support of the powerful War Veterans' Association, to head the heterogeneous company of the discontented and the ambitious. The coup d'état took place on 17 February 1936, Franco's party being known thereafter as Febreristas, 'men of February'. A strict press censorship was imposed; Eusebio Ayala, Estigarribia, and many prominent Liberals went into exile; and the Febreristas began belatedly to prepare a programme. The fundamental document of the régime, Decree No. 152, was published on 10 March. The preamble to this decree contained the announcement that 'the advent of the Liberating Revolution in Paraguay is of the same character as the totalitarian transformations occurring in contemporary Europe, in the sense that the Liberating Revolution and the State are now one and the same thing.' The decree placed a one-year ban on all activities of a political nature undertaken by party organizations, syndicates, and 'vested interests', unless they emanated explicitly from the Liberating Revolution, 'which is identical with the State'. The Ministry of the Interior was given permanent control in all social matters, such as labour disputes, the needs of workers and of capital, and all labour organizations and employers' associations.[1] Another decree created special tribunals to judge politicians who had been guilty of treachery during the war.[2] Colonel Franco proclaimed, furthermore, that he would expropriate land from the large estates for distribution among the landless poor, and during the short life of the régime a certain amount of land was so seized and allotted. Juan Stefanich, Franco's intelligent and idealistic Minister of Foreign Affairs, made a determined attempt to improve Paraguay's relations with neighbouring States, and before the fall of the Government he had signed friendly commercial agreements with Argentina, Brazil, and Uruguay.

The régime collapsed for three principal reasons. Firstly, Colonel Franco, in spite of his earlier protests that the Liberals had conceded too much to the Bolivians in the peace talks, felt obliged to agree to order the withdrawal of the Paraguayan

[1] Artaza, *Ayala*, pp. 155–7.   [2] ibid. p. 158.

troops from the advanced positions in the Chaco which they had held since the end of the war. Secondly, he dared not expropriate land belonging to foreign owners (chiefly Argentines), and he was thus unable to fulfil all his promises to the poor. Finally, the Liberals after the coup d'état of February 1936 did everything possible to foment revolution, and it is probable that they were implicated in the military rising which overthrew the Franco Government in August 1937. The Febreristas were defeated, but they had introduced a new element into politics. Future Governments would borrow from their programme for the creation of the 'New Paraguay'.

ESTIGARRIBIA AND THE CONSTITUTION OF 1940

Franco's fall was followed by two coups d'état and, thereafter, a brief period of internal peace under the presidency of a dean of the university. Then, in 1939, General Estigarribia, who had been adopted as the official Liberal candidate, was elected President of the Republic, and the second phase in the evolution of the New Paraguay began. Estigarribia soon found that his attempts to adhere to Liberal principles only served to encourage the revival of anarchy: his immediate restoration of political freedom had led to strikes, irresponsible attacks by the press, and conspiracies against the Government. He recognized that the revolutionary spirit which the Febreristas had aroused could not be suppressed and that Febrerista ideas must therefore be allowed to influence the course of national development. In February 1940, faced by increasing signs of social disorder, he declared himself temporarily dictator, with the assurance that the dictatorship would end as soon as a serviceable Constitution had been drawn up. Estigarribia now acted with great vigour, using the press and the radio to persuade the people of the need of a programme of State socialism on Febrerista lines. There is no reason to doubt his high motives or the distinterestedness of his patriotism. His plans—most of which he had not time to fulfil—included land expropriation, so that every landless Paraguayan family might be given a plot of its own; the building of highways, and of a pipeline to the oil-fields in the Bolivian Chaco; the creation of a merchant marine; monetary reform and, indeed, the general intervention of the State in social and economic matters.

Estigarribia's Constitution was successfully submitted to a plebiscite in August 1940. It is still in force today.

In the past the Constitutions of the majority of Latin American republics have been of little practical significance. A number of them, framed on the North American democratic model, have been to a large extent unworkable in Latin American circumstances, and therefore there has frequently occurred a contradiction between the nominal and the actual systems of government. 'It has been everywhere declared that the basis of state organization must be found in those conceptions of individual and collective freedom which inspired the theorists of the French Revolution. . . On the other hand in every one of the republics a very different régime has at times actually existed.'[1] Thus when considering the Government of most of these countries (there are, of course, several notable exceptions) little importance need be attached to their written Constitutions. The Paraguayan Constitution of 1940, however, is of another kind: it was deliberately designed as an adaptation of past and contemporary foreign theories and practices of government to the peculiar circumstances of the Mediterranean nation that Francia, the two López, and the Chaco War shaped and moulded. This Constitution is in the Paraguayan tradition; it is not an alien form imposed upon the country; and so, after its fashion, it serves the purpose for which it was conceived.

In an introduction, published with the text of the new Constitution, General Estigarribia explained that under the Constitution of 1870 the process of government worked too slowly and there was no provision for rapid action in emergencies. Paraguay, wrote the President, needed and would now be given 'a strong, but not a despotic, Executive'. The new Constitution would not create a totalitarian State, but would 'bring the democratic system to perfection'. The modern State must be more than a mere policeman: it must be equipped to deal at a moment's notice with social and economic problems, such as conflicts between capital and labour, sudden fluctuations in the national currency, the cornering of wealth, and artificial variations in prices. For this reason all administrative power must be concentrated in the hands of the Executive, with whom Parliament would collaborate in matters concerned with legislation. The modern State must be definitely nationalist, 'able to ensure social justice and to regulate the national life, without sacrificing the rights of the individual.' Briefly, 'the Executive must be given every possible

[1] Cecil Jane, *Liberty and Despotism in Spanish America* (Oxford, Clarendon Press, 1929), pp. 1–2.

power, but within the law.'[1] In other words, the authoritarian method of government, to which the Paraguayans for so long had been accustomed, was now to be accorded legal sanction.

Under the Constitution of 1940 the President of Paraguay is elected by direct suffrage for a period of five years, and can be re-elected for a second term. He is Commander-in-Chief of the armed forces of the Republic and is responsible for the country's relations with foreign Powers. He appoints the members of the Cabinet[2] and the holders of other administrative posts. In certain matters, such as the nomination of the Supreme Court and of diplomatic representatives, the President's decision must have the approval of an advisory body, the Council of State; but in practice this is a mere formality, especially since the majority of the Councillors are nominees of the President himself. The Council of State is composed of the Cabinet Ministers, the Rector of the University, the Archbishop of Paraguay, a representative of commerce, two representatives of agriculture, one representative of the processing industries, the President of the Central Bank, and representatives of the army and navy. The President of the Republic may, at his own discretion, dismiss Councillors of State. He is responsible for promotions in the armed forces. In times of emergency, internal or external, he may declare a state of siege throughout the Republic. While the state of siege is in operation, he may order the arrest of suspected persons or their removal from one part of the Republic to another. The President may dissolve the Chamber of Representatives, on condition that elections be held within two months of the dissolution. Article 54 of the Constitution establishes that

Proposals transmitted to the Chamber of Representatives by the Executive must be dealt with and disposed of during the sessions of that same year. If they are not disposed of during that period, they automatically become law. During the parliamentary recess, the Executive has the right to issue decrees which have the force of law, with the cognizance of the Council of State and the obligation to submit such laws to the Chamber of Representatives for approval in the next period of ordinary sessions.

---

[1] Ministerio de Gobierno y Trabajo, *Constitución de la República Paraguaya* (Asunción, 1940), pp. 5–15.

[2] There are ten Cabinet Ministers: Interior; Foreign Affairs and Worship; Finance; Education; Justice and Labour; National Defence; Public Health; Works and Communications; Agriculture and Livestock; Industry and Commerce.

The President has the right to veto bills passed by the Chamber.

The Chamber of Representatives is elected every five years by direct vote of the people, on the basis of one member for every 25,000 inhabitants. All male citizens who have reached the age of eighteen years have the right to vote; women voted for the first time in 1963. There is no upper House.

The judicial system consists of the Supreme Court, with three members; a Tribunal of Public Accounts; and the courts of first instance. The members of the Supreme Court are nominated by the President, with the approval of the Council of State. The members of the Tribunal of Public Accounts and all the other magistrates are appointed by the President, with the approval of the Supreme Court. The function of the Tribunal of Public Accounts is to examine administrative disputes and to watch over the expenditure of public funds.

The official religion is Roman Catholicism, but other religions are to be tolerated 'if they are not contrary to public morality and order'. The President is responsible for the appointment of the Archbishop and Bishops, in agreement with the Council of State and the Ecclesiastical Synod.

Other provisions of the Constitution (which, by Latin American standards, is unusually brief and concise) are as follows: primary education is obligatory and free; military service is compulsory for all male citizens; foreigners may obtain naturalization if they can prove that they have lived for five consecutive years in Paraguay and if they are owners of property or capital or are skilled in some science, art, or industry.

Three weeks after the promulgation of the Constitution President Estigarribia and his wife lost their lives in an aeroplane accident on the outskirts of Asunción. The Cabinet chose the Minister of War, General Higinio Morínigo, as Estigarribia's successor.

MORÍNIGO

The history of Paraguay from 1940 to 1948 can almost be reduced to the biography of the country's ruler. Higinio Morínigo ruled as absolutely as any of his predecessors, though more benevolently than most of them. In 1940, when the existing Cabinet nominated him temporarily to the presidency, he was forty-three years of age, an amiable and determined military officer possessing that typical Guaraní astuteness which, in Francisco Solano

López, had helped the Paraguayans to outwit their enemies for so long. In his eight years at the Government Palace, Morínigo was faced with the usual problems of his office. As far as possible he had to deflect the pressure exerted upon him by neighbouring States—and the United States, as a result of modern means of transport and new ideas of 'hemispheric defence', was now virtually an additional neighbour. He had to be constantly on his guard against conspiracies at home. And he had to try to improve the backward economy of his country, while knowing that the resources at his disposal were inadequate. In all these matters Morínigo was unexpectedly successful; and even after he had finally been driven into exile he remained for many years the most important figure in Paraguayan politics.

When he became 'temporary' President in 1940, the political scene was most confused and Morínigo himself had as yet no substantial body of supporters. He at once recognized that to remain in power he would at least have to satisfy an influential group of the young military leaders—he could not hope to please them all —who had gained rapid promotion during the Chaco War and who now felt that it was the destiny of the army to continue directing the affairs of the country whose independence it had saved on the battlefield. To many of these young officers it seemed that Estigarribia, in his attempt to build a bridge between 'up-to-date' totalitarianism and 'old-fashioned' Liberalism, had inclined too much in favour of the latter. Secondly, Morínigo had to deal with eager and impatient Febreristas—in and out of the army—who, as they had been the originators of the project for a 'New Paraguay', believed that they alone were fit to direct the future progress of the nation. Thirdly, the Cabinet contained four Liberal members who hoped to use Morínigo as a figurehead, while themselves controlling government policy: a prospect which he could not accept. Finally, the conservative Colorado Party, whom the Liberals had ousted as long ago as 1904 and who in recent years had refused to participate at all in politics, were still a force to be reckoned with; and they also had support in the higher ranks of the army. Morínigo could not afford to ignore them.

Morínigo's presidency began in the customary manner, with defections and attempted coups d'état. Within a few weeks of Estigarribia's death, the Liberals in the Cabinet, finding that the new President would not be subservient to their wishes, resigned and were replaced by military officers. Shortly afterwards General

Morínigo proclaimed that, in the interests of the nation, he felt obliged to assume 'the total responsibility of political power'. The Chamber of Representatives, he said, would not be allowed to meet again until he had changed the direction of the Paraguayan revolution. Many of the leading Liberals went into exile, while others were arrested. Several risings were attempted by Febreristas and by dissentient military factions, but they were all forcefully and speedily suppressed. In 1942, two years after Estigarribia's fatal accident, Morínigo announced that he had been asked by his military friends to remain in power for a further period of six years. Presidential elections were held at the beginning of 1943, with Higinio Morínigo as the only candidate.

All the foregoing happenings, and many others that followed, had the appearance, *mutatis mutandis*, of being a repetition of earlier Paraguayan history. But General Morínigo had one great advantage over his predecessors in the presidency: during most of his time in office the Second World War was in progress. The United States, fearful of Argentina's intentions and anxious to have a strategic base on the borders of that country, supplied Lend-Lease goods and money to Paraguay, financed the building of roads, and gave technical assistance in the development of agriculture and the health services. Brazil, Argentina's traditional rival, offered loans for public works and, like the United States, went out of its way to win Paraguayan friendship. The increased foreign demand for Paraguayan tinned meat, hides, cotton, quebracho, and petit-grain brought an unusual, though still moderate, prosperity. While remaining on the best of terms with Argentine military officers, and always mindful of Paraguay's dependence on Argentine transport and commercial finance, Morínigo extracted every possible advantage from the United States and Brazil. He paid official visits to both countries, being careful, when embarking on the long journey to Washington, to take with him his principal competitor in military-political circles, Colonel Benítez Vera, thus diminishing the chances of a rebellion during his absence. He also visited the President of Bolivia. At home, Morínigo protected his own position by allotting to the army—directly and indirectly—about 50 per cent of the national budget, thereby reducing the funds available for social services and education.

Throughout the war the North American and British authorities complained that Morínigo was too closely connected with pro-Axis officers at Buenos Aires and that he allowed German business firms, propagandists, and spies to work unhindered in Paraguay. These complaints, though understandable in the circumstances, were, from the Paraguayan point of view, inadmissible. Paraguay could not possibly have afforded to quarrel with Buenos Aires. The German Bank and the German School were important local institutions, and German colonists were among the most hard-working and productive members of the community. Moreover, the Allies were allowed approximately equal privileges with the Axis. The North American Protestant School, Allied propaganda services, and commercial houses continued to operate. To placate the United States and Great Britain, Morínigo severed diplomatic relations with the Axis countries. Later, he took nominal, and ineffectual, action to restrict the activities of the German Bank, School, commerce, and propaganda. At the eleventh hour, in February 1945, he declared war on the Axis and signed the Declaration of the United Nations. In March 1945 he signed the Act of Chapultepec and, in June of that year, the United Nations Charter. However, these actions did not mean that the President had adopted democratic principles. Indeed, the armaments that he received, in exchange, from the United States, helped him to woo the higher ranks of the Paraguayan army, who were pleased to receive them, and enabled him to suppress more easily the revolutions which from time to time threatened his continuance in office. Today many of the exiles who suffered severely under his rule concede that Morínigo, by and large, did serve the interests of Paraguay: unlike so many previous rulers, he maintained order; and he kept corruption within certain bounds. In making these admissions, none of Morínigo's opponents would pardon his harsh treatment of the Liberals, the Febreristas, the trade unions, and the press, or his offhand attitude to education and social welfare.

From the beginning of the war, the Paraguayan trade unions—which, although of comparatively recent growth, already had considerable influence in the meat-packing and tanning industries—were pro-Allied in sympathy and, for ideological as well as personal reasons, were opposed to Morínigo's dictatorship. A succession of strikes—some of them violent—soon caused the President to place all unions under Government control. The press and radio were likewise placed under the supervision of a government department—the Departamento Nacional de Propaganda (Denapro)—which was in effect a censorship office, while at the same time issuing instructions and official propaganda to the newspapers and broadcasting stations.

During Morínigo's rule, Colonel Franco and the leading Febreristas and Liberals spent most of their time in exile. The Communists—an active and resourceful, though not numerous, group—were also in exile, or worked 'underground' at home. The leading Colorados, though still bitterly anti-Liberal, demanded a return to parliamentary government. And, further to complicate the situation, three prominent pro-Axis officers—Colonels Benítez Vera, Bernardo Aranda, and Pablo Stagni—soon became so powerful in their respective positions at the cavalry garrison (Campo Grande) near Asunción, the General Staff headquarters in the capital, and the air base, that Morínigo was in danger of being completely dominated by them. In 1946, in self-defence, and employing his extraordinary astuteness, the President sent Colonel Benítez Vera on an official mission to Buenos Aires and seized the Colonel's garrison at Campo Grande during his absence. Aranda and Stagni thereupon fled to Argentina to join their out-manoeuvred colleague.

When the Allies had won the world war, Morínigo recognized that it would be wise to moderate his dictatorship. He declared a general amnesty, allowing political exiles to return to Paraguay, and persuaded some Colorados and Febreristas to join a coalition Government, on the understanding that elections would shortly be held. But the Paraguayans were still unprepared for democracy. A coup d'état against the régime was attempted in December 1946; the coalition government broke up in January 1947, and Morínigo had no alternative but to form yet another military Cabinet. In March 1947 civil war broke out in earnest. Colonel Franco was behind the insurgents, while the revolutionary committee consisted of Febreristas, Communists, and Liberals—an odd assortment, united in nothing except the desire to overthrow the President. During the civil war the Colorados backed Morínigo, who, when the rebels were finally defeated in August 1947, nominated the Colorado writer and publisher Natalicio González (in spite of the protests of the official party leaders) as the only presidential candidate in the long-promised elections. González was thus elected, together with an all-Colorado House of Representatives, in February 1948, and Paraguay became a one-party State. But the party was already split into those who accept-

ed Morínigo's leadership, and those who did not; and shortly
after the elections a group of Colorado military officers, who mis-
trusted him, forced Morínigo to leave the country. A number of
uprisings then occurred in quick succession, and Natalicio González himself was driven into exile, the Government finally passing into the hands of the rival Colorado faction, led by the veteran
Dr Frederico Chaves, who had the necessary military support.

Morínigo's rule and the immediate sequel have been described
at some length in this chapter because the present-day political
situation is a direct outcome of them. Morínigo maintained order,
but he drastically restricted individual liberties and his dictatorship created a political vacuum. His decision to fill that vacuum
by adopting the Colorado Party broke the party into two factions,
neither of which was sufficiently strong to remain in power without military aid; and so the traditional intervention of the army
in politics was perpetuated.

AFTER MORÍNIGO

The formalities of a presidential election were again performed
in February 1953, with Dr Chaves as the only candidate. On
14 August Paraguay officially adhered to the Argentine-Chilean
pact of 'economic union'. The document which Paraguay and
Argentina signed on that occasion expressed the desire for a
customs union and for the co-ordination of the economies of the
two countries, but it was primarily a bilateral trade and payments
agreement containing lists of products to be exchanged. A few
weeks later, to celebrate the signature of the pact, President
Perón visited Asunción; and his evident interest in Paraguayan
affairs caused some apprehension. In October 1953 Perón delivered a so-called 'Argentine-Paraguayan Decalogue' to a mass
meeting of his own compatriots at Buenos Aires, his principal
points being:

Every Argentine citizen should know that the Paraguayan people
and the Argentine people, fully retaining their national sovereignties,
are really and effectively brothers. Therefore, we Argentines must all
work for the greatness of Paraguay and for the happiness of its people
with the same faith and love as animate us when working for our own
greatness and happiness.

From today all Paraguayans will be compatriots of all Argentines.

Each one of us at his post must undertake to work to bring the Paraguayan and Argentine peoples together spiritually and materially.

The Government, the State, and the people of Argentina will make available all such resources and means as may help Paraguay to consolidate social justice, economic independence and political sovereignty.[1]

And so on. Trade between the two countries now increased, and it seemed that Argentina would provide financial and technical assistance for useful public works, such as the dredging of the port of Asunción.

But the aged President Chaves found that it was easier to come to an understanding with General Perón than to secure unity at home. At the beginning of May 1954 disagreement within the Colorado Party became so violent that the Commander-in-Chief of the armed forces, General Alfredo Stroessner, intervened. Superseding Dr Chaves, Stroessner became the official Colorado candidate for the presidency—and, therefore, the only candidate —in elections that were held in July. He was inaugurated President of the Republic on 15 August, and immediately afterwards General Perón again arrived in Asunción, bringing with him on this occasion the trophies captured from Paraguay by Argentina during the War of the Triple Alliance. These trophies—which included guns, flags, and church furniture—had been on exhibition in the Luján Museum, Buenos Aires. Perón declared that he was now returning them to Paraguay as a token of Argentina's desire to establish peace and friendship between the two nations. At Christmas 1954 Perón sent twenty-four truck-loads of gifts to the children of Paraguay. These gestures were appreciated. Furthermore, many Paraguayans were in agreement with Perón's social and economic policies, which they considered appropriate to contemporary South American circumstances. A new Paraguayan postage stamp was issued whereon the portraits of Stroessner and Perón appeared side by side.

The successful revolution against President Perón in September 1955 would in any case have had a profound effect on the policy of the Asunción Government; but the situation was aggravated by the fact that Perón, to avoid arrest by the revolutionary forces, sought refuge in a Paraguayan gunboat that happened to be lying in Buenos Aires harbour for repairs. The Argentine revolutionary Government respected the right of political asylum, in accordance with Latin American tradition; and at the beginning of October Perón was allowed to leave the gunboat and travel

[1] *Discursos de los Presidentes Chaves y Perón*, (Buenos Aires, Ministerio de Relaciones Exteriores y Culto, 1953), pp. 25–6.

to Paraguay by air. Nevertheless, the new authorities at Buenos Aires declared that the deposed President's continued residence at Asunción would be 'incompatible with the maintenance of harmonious relations between the two countries', and the Paraguayan Government were so dependent on Argentine economic collaboration that, in spite of their personal sympathy for Perón and his ideas, they could not ignore this implied threat. Perón was transferred to an estate in the interior, near Villarrica; and early in November he departed for Panama.

The problems created by Perón's presence in the Paraguayan gunboat and, afterwards, on Paraguayan soil, caused an intensification of the discord that already existed within the Colorado Party. The leadership of an anti-Stroessner faction of the Party was gradually assumed by the astute and efficient President of the Central Bank, Epifanio Méndez Fleitas, who had never concealed his Peronista convictions. Returning to Asunción in October 1955, after an official tour of Europe and the United States, Méndez Fleitas seemed to possess the diverse qualities that Paraguay needed in a ruler: he was an enlightened nationalist, a composer of Guaraní music; he had proved himself an able administrator at the Bank; and during his travels abroad he had studied the possibilities of attracting financial and technical aid and had already made considerable progress to that end. In December, following an abortive insurrection, Méndez Fleitas was relieved of his office.[1]

[1] For brief references to these events, see the Asunción newspaper *La Tribuna*, 23 and 24 December 1955, and President Stroessner's Christmas message, ibid. 25 December 1955.

Chapter VI

STROESSNER

PRESIDENT Stroessner ruled with a firm hand; he maintained a state of siege more or less permanently (renewing it every 60 days, so as formally to comply with the requirements of the Constitution); his police arrested political opponents when they threatened to cause trouble, and suppressed student demonstrators; and his army (whose officers were a favoured class) ruthlessly crushed any attempts by exiled Febreristas and Liberals to stir up revolution, as in 1959, when bands of guerrillas from Argentina and Brazil crossed the Río Paraná and held out for a short while in the forests of the littoral.

By maintaining political order in this forceful manner, Stroessner created conditions in which he could proceed with a programme of economic reconstruction and development, attracting foreign aid and investment, building roads through the forests, settling families on fertile, unexploited lands, and so on.

In 1956 Stroessner invited a team from the International Monetary Fund to reform the currency system. In 1957—under IMF advice, and with IMF and U.S. Treasury backing—Paraguay completely abandoned its elaborate methods of exchange and trade control. Credit restrictions and wage controls were introduced; taxes were raised; public spending was reduced. As a result of these various measures, the guaraní became one of the most stable currencies in South America and the cost of living, which had risen vertiginously in previous years, was held in check.

Meanwhile, to indicate its disapproval of Stroessner's previously cordial relations with Perón, the Argentine revolutionary Government temporarily withheld the implementation of the trade agreements that Perón had negotiated with Paraguay. Argentina's coolness provided Brazil with the opportunity to reaffirm its own concern for Paraguay's welfare, and, particularly, regarding its need for an alternative outlet to the sea. In October 1956 Stroessner met the Brazilian President, Kubitschek, at the little town of Foz do Iguassu, on the Brazilian bank of the Río Paraná, where they then laid the foundation stone of an international bridge over the river.

This bridge, now completed, joins the Paraguayan road system with the Brazilian highway that leads to the Atlantic coast at Paranaguá, where Paraguay has free-zone facilities. Brazil provided assistance for the completion and improvement of the Paraguayan road to the bridge. United States aid for a number of public works continued.

In 1958 Stroessner was re-elected to the presidency by a plebiscite in which he was the Colorados' (and the only) candidate; the sixty members of the Chamber of Deputies elected at the same time were also affiliated to the Colorado Party, the only political organization permitted. At the next elections, those of 1963, however, Stroessner, for the sake of democratic appearances, permitted (or persuaded) a splinter-group of the Liberal Party to play the rôle of opposition, on the understanding that, although they would of course be defeated at the polls, they would automatically be granted one-third of the seats in the Chamber. This so-called Renovación faction of the Liberal Party (bitterly repudiated by the Liberals in exile) adopted Ernesto Gavilán as its presidential candidate. Defeated at the elections, Gavilán was rewarded with the post of Ambassador to Britain; the Renovacionistas duly received their twenty seats in the Chamber.

The Renovacionistas justified their virtual collaboration with the Colorado Party on the grounds that the Colorados had now become 'reformists', and that their policies no longer differed greatly from those of the Liberals. It was argued that the Stroessner régime was in fact one-party rule, rather than a personal dictatorship. Certainly Stroessner himself 'had not the appearance of an old style pistol-packing military tyrant'. On the contrary, he was 'mild-looking and almost diffident in his talk; not the fireball demagogic type who can inflame an audience with a forceful platform manner'.[1] Anyway, the Colorados held a tight grip on all the departments of state, and Stroessner was a hardworking leader of government.

[1] Edward C. Burke, *New York Times*, 18 February 1964.

Chapter VII

THE PEOPLE AND THEIR OCCUPATIONS, I

THE POPULATION

At the time of the census of 1962 the population of Paraguay was about 1,817,000,[1] including the inhabitants of the Paraguayan Chaco, who numbered only about 50,000. According to official estimates, in recent years there have been approximately 30 births and 10 deaths per 1,000 inhabitants per annum; infant mortality is about 100 per 1,000 births.[2] Vital statistics, however (and other statistics too) are unreliable. In the country districts births often go unregistered, and deaths of very young children are not always recorded. An example of the unreliability of the official birth statistics appeared in 1942–3 in the village and district of Piribebuy, about forty-six miles south-east of the capital:

> The number of births registered each year in the district of Piribebuy in the decade ending with 1942 varied from about 300 to 500, except in 1942 when it was 922. This increase was probably due to the fact that the cost of registration and fines for late registrations were remitted in that year. Actually only one-fourth of the 922 births occurred in 1942; the others were for births many years in the past, some as far away as 1887. It was noted that registration of births was often delayed; 1942 births continued to be recorded in the 1943 register until August 1943 when birth registrations during that year ceased because a needed registration book was not sent from Asunción.[3]

In the same district it was found that during the period 1942–4 296 children had been baptized who were not on the civil register. The state of affairs has not materially changed in the meantime.

Over 50 per cent of the births in Paraguay are illegitimate. This high rate of illegitimacy is usually explained by, first, the great distance which separates many of the rural dwellings from the nearest town; second, the poverty of the peasants, who cannot afford the expense of the marriage ceremony; and, third, the

---

[1] For further population figures see App. I, p. 84.
[2] Presidencia de la República, *Cuentas nacionales de la República del Paraguay*, Vol. III (Asunción, Secretaría Técnica de Planificación, 1964).
[3] Emma Reh, *Paraguayan Rural Life* (Washington, Institute of Inter-American Affairs, Food Supply Division, 1946), pp. 18–19.

excess of women in the urban centres. Marriage may be performed both as a civil and as a religious ceremony. By law the religious service is allowed only after the civil ceremony has been performed, but the law is sometimes disregarded and the civil ceremony omitted. Divorce and remarriage are not allowed.

According to Emma Reh, who was responsible for the detailed study of Piribebuy, and whose comments are still widely applicable today,

> Of all the single women in the population, 41 per cent have children, 17 per cent live with their children in their parents' home, 16 per cent have homes alone with their children, and 8 per cent live in free unions... The unfavourable aspect of this situation is the economic and social disorganization of family life which results.[1]

In Piribebuy nearly one family in every three is incomplete, with a woman at the head.

> The household headed by women, it is often explained in Paraguay, was common and necessary after the war of 1870 when most fighting men were killed and even women, as in the battle of Piribebuy, went to war. When, after a generation, the balance of sexes was largely re-established and this mode of living was no longer necessary, it continued from habit.[2]

As has already been mentioned, immigration has always been spasmodic and, by South American standards, slight.

On the other hand, emigration has been substantial. Many thousands of Paraguayans have been attracted to the more prosperous and less disturbed nearby regions of Argentina and Brazil. Others have settled in those countries, and in Uruguay, to escape political persecution at home. It is estimated that at least 150,000 heads of family, most of them accompanied by their wives and children, emigrated from Paraguay during the period 1904–23, and the numbers probably increased thereafter. It is considered that between 500,000 and 600,000 Paraguayans, with their families, are now living in Argentina and Brazil.

Statistics of immigration and emigration are incomplete, however, and many people have entered and left the country unrecorded. Like the *contrabandistas* who abound in the riverside towns of Argentina, Brazil, and Paraguay, political fugitives have little difficulty in secretly crossing the river frontiers.

[1] Emma Reh, *Paraguayan Rural Life*, p. 22.
[2] ibid. p. 24. Miss Reh does not accept this explanation.

The People and their Occupations, I

In addition to the mainly *mestizo* population of Paraguay, the few remaining tribes of indigenous Indians, and the relatively small foreign communities in Asunción and the provincial towns, several foreign colonies have been established in the interior of the republic in recent times, one of the most successful being the Mennonite settlement in the Chaco, to the west of Puerto Casado. The Mennonite wanderers, seeking a country where they might practise their religion in peace, acquired a tract of land of more than 320,000 acres in this region, and the first settlers began to arrive, from Canada, early in 1927. The Paraguayan Government accorded them virtual self-rule, generous concessions in regard to tariffs and taxation, unrestricted immigration facilities, and perpetual exemption from military service. By April 1927 about 2,000 Mennonites had already settled in the colony. Others came from eastern Europe, Russia, Manchuria, and North America, until in 1933 the colonists numbered 5,000. Like the earlier 'Lincolnshire Farmers' and Lane's Australian followers, the Mennonites suffered many hardships, and desertions occurred. Smaller groups set themselves up in other parts of the country. The Chaco War nearly engulfed the original settlement. But the Mennonites survived all these troubles. They worked hard, developed their agriculture, cattle-raising, and manual crafts, and are today a valuable element in the life of the country which granted them asylum. Their isolation has been relieved by the trans-Chaco road, which now joins their settlement of Filadelfia with Villa Hayes, on the west bank of the Río Paraguay, some twenty miles north of Asunción.

At the beginning of the Second World War the Hutterite brethren, who came chiefly from Great Britain and Germany, acquired a tract of 20,000 acres north-east of Asunción where they founded a colony rather similar to those of the Mennonites, naming it Primavera, but this colony disbanded in 1962.

Several German and Japanese colonies have long been established in Paraguay.

From the beginning of his régime General Stroessner concentrated on the construction of roads, one of his principal aims being to open up the fertile but thinly populated regions bordering the Upper Paraná River for colonization, and there, as the road-building progressed, the Instituto de Bienestar Rural (a government agency) launched a scheme for distributing land to colonists. People were encouraged to move out from the more crowded

49

central districts of the Republic; and when the stability of the Stroessner régime became more apparent, some of the Paraguayan families who had emigrated to the other side of the Paraná were attracted back to their own country—one of the colonies in which they were settled was named Colonia Repatriación.

Meanwhile Japanese settlers were entering the Paraná region under an agreement signed by the Paraguayan Government in 1959 which provided for the admission of 85,000 immigrants from Japan during the following thirty years, the maximum annual quota being fixed at 3,500.

TOWN AND COUNTRY

Life in Paraguay is predominantly rural. Only about 15 per cent of the population live in the capital city proper. The majority of Paraguayans grow most of their own food, and it is probable that at least 70 per cent of the families in the smaller towns farm land for themselves, though many have additional occupations, earning wages in town, or running small businesses of their own. There is a shortage of skilled workers such as carpenters and mechanics, partly because, for many years, skilled labour was better rewarded in Argentina, and went there.

The most intensively cultivated region in Paraguay is the country around Asunción; and although this agricultural zone amounts to only about 5 per cent of the total area of the Republic, it contains about 60 per cent of the total population. Outside this zone the land is sparsely populated and the inhabitants rely more on livestock and forest exploitation for a living than on farming.

Asunción is the seat of government, the main river port, the hub of the road system that covers south-eastern Paraguay, and the point of departure of the (now very decrepit) railway to Encarnación and Buenos Aires. About 90 per cent of the country's imports and exports pass through the capital. The city is governed by a mayor, who is appointed by the President of the Republic, and an elected Council. In the central district of the capital are several public buildings erected during the régimes of Carlos Antonio López and his son (the Congressional Palace, the cathedral, the Government Palace, and the railway station), a National Pantheon (containing the remains of López and Estigarribia), and a number of modern buildings, such as that of the Bank of the Republic. The principal thoroughfares and the central commercial streets are asphalted, but the lesser streets are still paved with cobble-stones. Many streets are lined with orange trees. The residential houses are mostly of one storey, built of plastered brick, with whitewashed or pale yellow or pink façades, tiled roofs, grilled windows, and verandas that are festooned with vines and flowering creepers. The older residences have patios, but the newer houses are more often of the chalet type, similar in style to the chalets of the modern suburbs of other Latin American capitals. Patios and gardens throughout Asunción are gay with flowering shrubs and trees—bougainvillia, magnolia, jasmine, hibiscus, gardenia, roses, and the national tree, the lapacho, which has pink or purple blossoms. Grape-fruit trees flourish in the garden of López's favourite residence, which is now the Gran Hotel del Paraguay (Mme Lynch's private theatre is the hotel dining-room), and mango trees fill the courtyard of one of the principal military establishments. There are two luxuriant parks overlooking the river. Orchids grow on the trees in the botanical gardens.

From the higher floors of Asunción's new Hotel Guaraní (one of the finest hotels in South America), you look down upon the town's red roofs and the vegetation (which remains green all the year round); in the distance, you can see the powerful Río Paraguay, flowing past the town; and *beyond* the river, you see the flat shore of the Chaco—the two Paraguays, from one window.

Paraguay's provincial towns are entrepôts for the rural regions. Encarnación, on the Río Paraná, is the port from which the products of a rich area (timber, *yerba*, cotton, and tobacco) are shipped downstream; and Encarnación and the Argentine town of Posadas, on the opposite side of the Paraná, are the two ports for the ferry which conveys the international train across the river on its long journeys between Asunción and Buenos Aires. Encarnación is also the centre from which the Jesuit ruins of Trinidad and Jesús are visited. The town of Concepción, situated on the River Paraguay, is the entrepôt of the north, having considerable trade with Brazil. Revolutions have often begun at Concepción, with the local garrison rising against the Asunción Government. Villarrica, about midway on the railway between Asunción and Encarnación, is the centre for the collection of produce from a fertile district—tobacco, cotton, sugar, and *yerba*—and wine produced by the nearby German colony.

In the provincial towns and the villages the only old buildings that have survived are situated in and around the main plaza, which is covered with fine, closely-cropped grass. They usually consist of a whitewashed church, with pillared verandas extending the full length of the outer walls; one-storey homes built along one side of the square in a solid row beneath a single roof which overhangs to form a veranda along the whole façade of the block; and perhaps one or two moderately spacious residences with tiled roofs, brick floors, balconies, patios, flowering vines, and a well.

Outside the central area of Asunción and the other towns most of the workers still live in small huts made of mud and reeds, with earth floors and communal wells. In the country districts almost all the dwellings are of this rancho type. They provide inadequate shelter in rainy weather and are doubtless partly responsible for the prevalence of colds and influenza in winter. Pneumonia and influenza are the two chief causes of death in Paraguay. Brick and plaster houses are becoming more common, however, especially in the towns that can now be reached by the new highways; and recent Governments have displayed some interest in schemes for better housing for urban and rural workers. Nevertheless, although roads are still few, the rural people are not so isolated as this fact might suggest. They are for ever coming and going. The young men travel in search of work on ranches, in timber camps, on river boats, and so on. In particular, they visit Asunción. 'It seems that nearly everyone—men, women, children, rich and poor—manages to get to Asunción occasionally for one reason or another.'[1] Another cause of rural mobility is politics. In any locality are to be found men who are virtually political refugees, having left their home town because they once backed the wrong political group. Dr and Mrs Service consider that this habitual movement of people from district to district may have contributed to the Paraguayans' racial and cultural homogeneity.

For administrative purposes Paraguay is divided into sixteen departments, each of which is governed by a delegate appointed by the President of the Republic. Each department is divided into municipalities and rural districts named *partidos*. The *partidos*, in turn, are subdivided into *compañias*. The district of Piribebuy can be taken as representative of eastern Paraguay:

The *compañias* are separated from one another by trails, gullies, hills or other physical features. They differ in size and vary in population from

[1] E. R. and H. S. Service, *Tobatí* (University of Chicago Press, 1954), p. 19.

perhaps 50 to 200 families. The *compañías* have *Guaraní* Indian names descriptive in nature, and have their own recognized sub-divisions, or *parajes* which also have *Guaraní* names.

Districts and *compañías* are functioning groups. People in them feel and are related...

The district or *partido* of Piribebuy is governed by a number of officials, of whom the strongest is the *comisario*, or police chief, who is appointed by the national government in Asunción or its agent in the Department... The *comisario* enforces the law, makes arrests, and keeps order. He has an assistant *comisario* and ten subalterns, who are conscripts under 20 years old in army uniform and with army pay... The *comisario* carries out orders coming from the central government in Asunción as well as orders made by the *junta* or municipal council in the town of Piribebuy. This *junta* has five members who are residents of the town but are appointed directly by the Department of the Interior in Asunción with the advice of influential local merchants and other important persons. Council members serve without pay...

In 1945 the Piribebuy *junta* included a former colonel in the army who was also one of the town's richest farmers, the village doctor, who was a European refugee, one of the two town bakers, a school teacher, and a carpenter who was born in Italy. They represented both sides in the political ideology of World War II. The *junta* elects one of its members *presidente municipal*; in Piribebuy in 1945 this was the former colonel who had already served six years, or ever since municipal elections were suspended in Paraguay. The *presidente's* pay is 6 per cent of the 5,000 *guaraníes*[1] which the Asunción government allows the Piribebuy council to levy in the district in a year.

Next to the *comisario* and the *presidente municipal*, the judge who is appointed by the Department of Justice in Asunción is the most important person in the town or district. He settles local controversies and tries and sentences accused persons. He is an outsider, but his assistant is from Piribebuy. There are other employees of the central government in Piribebuy: an internal revenue collector, two agents of the Agricultural Bank, and a postmaster-telegraph operator...

The director of schools, an important position in a district, is often a woman.[2]

SOCIAL SERVICES

Foreign nutrition experts consider that the diet of the poorer classes in Paraguay is deficient, but local doctors usually claim that it is adequate. Paraguay is a great meat-eating country, mainly beef.[3] In rural districts mandioca takes the place of bread. This starchy root is grown by all farming families. It is best liked

[1] The guaraní was at that time worth approximately U.S. 33 cents.
[2] Reh, *Paraguayan Rural Life*, pp. 14–16.   [3] ibid. p. 81.

freshly boiled and is also used, after grinding, in the making of the special Paraguayan cakes called *chipá*. Maize is another universal crop, and maize flour is in general use, though wheat, mostly imported from Argentina, is milled in Asunción for urban consumption. The most popular beverage is *mate*, which is made by pouring boiling water on the toasted leaves of the *yerba* tree, native to the forests of eastern Paraguay. The dairy industry is small, but in 1943 STICA (Servicio Técnico Interamericano de Cooperación Agrícola)[1] established a model farm at San Lorenzo near Asunción which has encouraged milk production. The supposed lack of calcium in the Paraguayan diet is one of the deficiencies referred to by nutritionists.

The United States has not only provided technical and financial aid for the improvement of local agricultural methods and equipment, but has also helped in the work of expanding and modernizing the health services. The Servicio Cooperativo Interamericano began to operate in 1942 with a technical staff appointed by the Institute of Inter-American Affairs of Washington. Under the guidance of a particularly active North American director, Dr Richard J. Plunkett, the mission drew up a public health programme, special attention being given to tuberculosis and leprosy. Tuberculosis was found to be the chief cause of death in Asunción, but there were only about seventy hospital beds available for tubercular patients in the capital, and none in the country. One of the Servicio Cooperativo's first projects, therefore, was the construction of a sanatorium on the outskirts of the city. The Bella Vista Sanatorium was inaugurated and turned over to the Paraguayan Government in 1945. It was directed by an able Paraguayan physician of French-German descent, Dr Juan Max Boettner, who was also a distinguished pianist and composer.

Another early undertaking by the Servicio Cooperativo was the erection, two miles outside Asunción, of the Santa Teresita Preventorium for children whose parents suffer from leprosy. This project was inspired by a public-spirited woman, Señora Eloisa Talavera de Taboada, wife of a former Cabinet Minister. Señora Taboada had visited a leper settlement at Sapucay and had been shocked to discover that uninfected children were living at the colony because their parents were there. She quickly won the support of Dr Plunkett, and an isolation centre was built, and pre-

[1] See below, p. 62.

sented to the State, where such children could receive academic and vocational training.

Most of Paraguay's hospitals and medical facilities are concentrated in Asunción and the other towns. A few regional rural hospitals have been established in recent years, however, and the number of trained doctors and nurses is increasing.

Social insurance was first established in 1943 by a decree-law which created the Instituto de Previsión Social (Social Welfare Institute) and made insurance compulsory for all persons up to sixty years of age. This was modified in 1950 by decree-law no. 1860 whereby insurance became obligatory for salary- and wage-earners of any age 'working under a written or oral contract of employment', and for apprentices not receiving wages. The scheme does not apply to civil servants and railway employees, who have special insurance funds of their own—the Caja Nacional de Jubilaciones Civiles and the Caja de Jubilaciones y Pensiones de Empleados Ferroviarios respectively. The insurance of self-employed persons and of workers who have no contract of employment is not compulsory but may be undertaken voluntarily on application to the national Institute.

The Institute is an autonomous body and is administered by a Superior Council and a Director-General, who is the chairman of the Council. The Director-General is appointed by the Executive, the other six members of the Council being: 1 representative of the Ministry of Health, 1 representative of the Ministry of Justice and Labour, 2 representatives of the employers, and 2 representatives of the insured persons.

The national insurance scheme provides for free medical attention (which is not yet always available) and subsidies during illness or when suffering from injury, payment of maternity expenses and a nine weeks' grant to mothers, old-age pensions at the age of sixty, and burial expenses. This expenditure is financed by a levy on salaries and wages, employers paying 13 per cent, employees 6 per cent, and the State $1\frac{1}{2}$ per cent.

Unemployment insurance does not exist, but compensation is payable to employees on dismissal, on the basis of length of service.

The National Department of Labour, which is responsible to the Ministry of Justice and Labour, is concerned with the settlement of disputes between labour and capital and the registration and control of all syndicates. The Department has a board composed of a president, a secretary, three councillors, a representative of the employers, and a representative of the workers. The resolutions of this board are binding upon employers and workers alike. The National Department of Labour has the power to fix minimum wages. Working hours were fixed in 1938 by a decree which established a maximum of 8 hours a day or 48 hours a week for normal work, and a maximum of 6 hours a day or 36 hours a week for young persons under the age of sixteen and for unhealthy work. Contracts may be drawn up between employers and workers increasing the maximum of 8 hours to a maximum of 10 hours a day, on condition that a wage increase of 50 per cent is paid for the overtime. The maximum hours do not apply to agricultural labourers or domestic servants.

Workers' syndicates, of which there are about ninety, must have the approval of the National Department of Labour. Most of these syndicates are affiliated to the Confederación Paraguaya de Trabajadores, which has Government backing, and belongs to the continental Asociación de Trabajadores Latino-Americanos (ATLAS). Industrial employers are organized in a body called La Unión Industrial Paraguaya. Strikes and lockouts are illegal unless authorized by the Department of Labour.

It is not surprising that a nation which for so many years has devoted so much of its energies to war and revolution should be backward in educational matters. Countless university professors and school-teachers, whom the nation could ill afford to lose, have gone into exile, never to return, and students have become active politicians long before completing their studies. The result is a general retardment in educational development which many disinterested and devoted men and women in recent decades have struggled to remedy. Successive Governments, while recognizing the need for more schools and qualified teachers, have failed, however, to provide sufficient funds for improvement on a large scale.

One of the fundamental problems is neither political nor financial. As the Paraguayan child usually speaks Guaraní at home, his first contact with his native land's official tongue—Spanish—is in the primary school. All the school books are in Spanish, so the pupil must learn the language. But he continues to *think* in Guaraní. His school work is a translation.

Primary education, which is free, is nominally compulsory from the age of seven to fourteen; but in practice thousands of children never attend school and illiteracy is widespread. It is estimated that even in Asunción 15 per cent of the inhabitants above seven years of age are illiterate and that outside the capital 40 per cent are illiterate. It has been calculated that nearly 42 per cent of the children of school age do not attend school. The reasons for the non-attendance of so many children are numerous. The nearest school may be too far from home or it may already be full. The children may have to go to work to help support the family, or their parents may themselves be too ignorant to appreciate the value of education. Some children of poor families who wish to attend cannot afford the white smock, the book, slate, paper, pen, ink, and pencil which are obligatory. Emma Reh noted

> School is esteemed by children and truancy is rare. . . Children from the *compañías* walk miles to the town school every day; boys walking from the distant *compañías* to the morning session have to get up long before dawn to get to school at eight. They eat a hard biscuit or piece of mandioca on their way.[1]

In the curriculum of primary schools prominence is given to practical training in manual crafts such as gardening, cooking, and weaving. This useful branch of education is sometimes hampered by the lack of equipment. Most primary schools are run by the State, but some private secondary schools have primary classes.

Before beginning their secondary studies pupils who have completed the primary course must do an additional year of higher studies. The secondary course has two parts: a five-year course leading to a bachelor in science or letters certificate, and a final pre-university year. About half of the secondary schools (*colegios*) are State owned. The principal private schools—all of them in Asunción—are the Colegio San José (Catholic), the Colegio Internacional (run by North American Protestants), and the German school, which came under rather perfunctory State supervision in the later months of the Second World War.

Primary teachers are trained in lower normal schools (*escuelas normales de maestros*) whose four-year courses are at the secondary level. A further three-year course is given at the *escuelas normales de profesores* for preparing secondary school teachers. There are a number of vocational and technical schools, some of which are under the Ministries of Agriculture and Health.

In 1963 the National University at Asunción had 3,765 students

[1] Reh, *Paraguayan Rural Life*, pp. 42–43.

(mostly men) and 499 teachers. The Faculty of Law and Social Science continued to be the most popular (895 students), followed by that of Economic Science (643 students.)[1] Many Paraguayans have completed their higher studies in Buenos Aires or, with North American scholarships, in the United States. Before the Second World War several medical doctors who became prominent in Asunción studied in Germany.

[1] Presidencia de la República, *Cuentas nacionales*, iii, 1964.

Chapter VIII

THE PEOPLE AND THEIR OCCUPATIONS, II

AGRICULTURE

THE most important single event in the modern development of Paraguayan agriculture was the creation of STICA[1] with its United States experts, up-to-date equipment, improved seeds, etc., in 1942–3. The beneficial effects of STICA's example and teaching are apparent today on many farms and ranches; nevertheless, throughout a vast area of the country, where that influence has not yet penetrated, agricultural conditions have not greatly changed since Charles A. Washburn visited Paraguay in the early 1860's:

> In front or in the rear of the house is a cultivated field, seldom of more than two or three acres in extent, and yet in this field will be raised all that the family has to consume for the year. There will be a patch of Indian corn, another of sugar-cane, another of cotton, another of mandioca, and another of tobacco; but the whole aggregate would seldom exceed two acres in extent, and on the produce thus raised the family would mainly subsist for a year. The cattle which belonged to the different occupants grazed in common on the plains in front, and each family would have a sufficient number of cows to supply it with all the milk required. They would have likewise a number of chickens; and as the cattle were very cheap, beef was always to be had at the market of the capilla at a very low price. About the only article that was counted a luxury by the Paraguayans was the *yerba maté*, and it was for the purchase of this more than any other, that they parted with anything that they had raised on their little patches. The tobacco which they grew was always in demand, and would command money in Asuncion; and it was from the money realized from this crop principally that the inhabitants purchased the much-coveted *maté*. Something also was required for the purchase of imported muslins, handkerchiefs, and shawls by the women, and for some articles of clothing worn by the men; but the amount of clothing worn was so very little that the cost of it was very light.[2]

An agricultural census undertaken between 1942 and 1944 showed that there were 94,498 *chacras*, or farms, in which at least

---

[1] See below, p. 62.   [2] Washburn, *History of Paraguay*, vol. 1, pp. 432–3.

1 hectare[1] was cultivated. The average area of cultivated land per
farm was 3·5 hectares. There were in addition about 26,000 small
holdings with less than 1 hectare cultivated.[2] One of the reasons
for the large number of small properties is that the custom of
primogeniture is not observed in Paraguay: on the death of the
owner the land is divided among the heirs in equal portions.
Often, so that each plot may have access to a road, the subdivi-
sion is made in long narrow strips which are inconvenient for
working. The census of 1942–4 revealed, however, that less than
one-fifth of the farmers were proprietors of the land they worked;
even fewer paid rent; most were simply *ocupantes*, squatters, with
or without permission, paying neither rent nor taxes. Over 60 per
cent of those surveyed came into this last category.[3] In the interior
of the country it is common for a farmer to abandon a plot of land
when he has begun to exhaust its fertility, and to move elsewhere,
clearing a new patch of the jungle by *machete* and fire. Thus in the
more remote parts of Paraguay farming, paradoxically, is almost
nomadic.[4] The wooden ox-drawn plough is still widely used.

It has long been accepted that one of the basic requirements
of Paraguayan agriculture is that farmers should be provided with
land of their own. The first comprehensive legislation for this purpose was introduced by Colonel Franco in May 1936. The law of
that date authorized the Government to expropriate 5 million
acres, to pay for it with bonds, and to sell it to farmers in plots of
25 to 250 acres. These reforms were to be supervised by a Consejo
de Reforma Agraria. Instruction in the rudiments of husbandry
was declared obligatory in all schools. In 1940 President Estigarribia signed a National Agrarian Statute which was designed to
carry the reforms even further.[5] The avowed object of the statute
was to ensure that every Paraguayan family would own the land
upon which it dwelt and that its piece of land would be adequate
to provide the family with 'all the necessaries of life'. The Departmento de Tierras y Colonización was made responsible for the
redistribution of land, official and private colonization, the re-

[1] 1 hectare = 2·471 acres.
[2] *Censo de Agricultura del Paraguay*, published jointly by the Paraguayan
Ministerio de Agricultura and the Institute of Inter-American Affairs (Asunción, 1948).
[3] ibid. p. 72.
[4] Milan Cirovic, 'El Nomadismo Agrícola en el Paraguay', *Cultura* (Asunción),
July 1947.
[5] *Cf.* Carlos Pastore's *La Lucha por la Tierra en el Paraguay* (Montevideo,
Antequera, 1949). Sr Pastore drew up the National Agrarian Statute of 1940.

patriation of Paraguayan families from abroad, the selection and control of immigrants, and the development and defence of the natural resources of the country. Land could be granted to male Paraguayans above the age of eighteen, women with families to support, foreigners intending to engage in agriculture, and agrarian communities of a certain size. The lands to be distributed were public lands not required for other purposes, private land in the vicinity of communities needing it for expansion, and any private land suitable for agriculture not 'rationally exploited' by its owners. In the eastern part of the country 'rational exploitation' meant that at least half the estate must be under cultivation. The maximum and minimum sizes to be distributed were fixed. The redistribution of land in accordance with this statute was of course unpopular amongst the landowners, and the constant fear of expropriation was probably detrimental to production. In August 1953 the authorities announced a new plan which was a tacit admission that the policy of dividing farms into small holdings had been a failure. In future, instead of redistributing the land, certain parts of the cattle ranches would be systematically colonized with the agreement, and under the direction, of the owners, who would still remain in possession.

With the years, programmes for land reform have been altered and extended; and, in addition, the Government has introduced other measures intended to increase agricultural production. For example, farmers who undertake to sow a specified area have been granted special credit terms, and minimum prices have been guaranteed for the basic crops.

It is difficult to assess the results of these various measures, but the total area under cultivation has certainly risen.

Dr and Mrs Service are not convinced that land ownership is a vital problem in Paraguay at the present time.

To say that over three-fourths of the Paraguayan agriculturalists are landless is not to say the same thing that might be implied in a similar statement about other countries. The Paraguayan is often landless only in the sense that he holds no legal title to his plot; he usually has access to more land than he can cultivate with his primitive equipment. His problem is basically that of the whole nation; he is virtually without a market for his product and consequently without capital. . . . For the Paraguayan peasant to hold title to the plot he occupies confers no economic benefit and might be actually a liability, in the sense that it would tend to tie him to increasingly less productive land, when, by moving, he could find a more fertile location. A typical Paraguayan rural area such as Tobatí is not excessively primitive or poor, however, as compared with isolated rural areas in other Latin-American countries. What is striking is the fact that the whole nation is more backward than most other Latin-American nations.[1]

The Institute of Inter-American Affairs at Washington and the Paraguayan Government jointly founded the Servicio Técnico Interamericano de Cooperación Agrícola in December 1942, both parties contributing financially. The immediate purpose of the organization was to stimulate the production of food and raw materials needed by the North Americans and their allies in the war; but the service continued after the cessation of hostilities, as a branch of the Paraguayan Ministry of Agriculture. Its activities include the running of an Institute of Agronomy, an experimental farm, a model ranch and dairy farm, and the provision of technical advice. Particular attention has been given to the improvement of seeds, storage and the introduction of new crops, weed-control and the use of fertilizers, insecticides, and modern agricultural machinery. STICA collaborates in the organization of new national colonies established under the various land reform projects.

One of the most important innovations recommended by STICA was the creation of an agency to provide agrarian credit. For this purpose the Crédito Agrícola de Habilitación (CAH) was set up in December 1943, its principal functions being the granting of credit to small farmers and the education of selected farmers in modern agricultural methods. Credits were to be authorized on the basis of personal reports prepared by 'rural supervisors', trained by STICA, who would visit the farmers and their families. To qualify for a loan a farmer had to be of good character, experienced in farm work, and likely to develop his holding and pay off the debt. The amount of credit granted depended on the productive capacity of the holding and on an estimate of how much could be accomplished during the term of the loan. The domestic organization of the household was also taken into account, and women supervisors gave advice on managing the home, and feeding and clothing the family. Loans were granted for various terms: for one year for current expenses, buying seeds and fertilizers; for five years for the purchase of tools, machinery, and stock; for ten or

[1] E. R. and H. S. Service, *Tobatí*, pp. 295–6.

fifteen years for major improvements to the holding and for buying new land. Interest was originally fixed at 6 per cent but the maximum was later raised.

STICA's achievements in the first twenty years of its existence were far from negligible, but they were strictly limited. When a new STICA plan was published in 1962, it showed that all the familiar old problems were still to be tackled. Thus STICA reported that about 50 per cent of the agricultural workers in Paraguay were still *ocupantes*:

they simply occupy land that belongs to the State or to private owners; there, they construct their shack with sticks and mud, cultivate a small fraction of the land for their own subsistence, and when the fertility of the soil has been exhausted and the shack is falling to pieces they abandon the site and move on, to repeat the process elsewhere.

In 1962, the report continued, there was still

an almost total absence of credits for assisting the farmer to increase his production. The private Banks do not provide credits to farmers, and only grant them occasionally to *estancieros*. Because it lacked the financial means, the Crédito Agrícola de Habilitación (CAH) ceased operations. There is substantial evidence of a decline in rural capital in recent years. Occasionally merchants do give credit to farmers, but at exorbitant rates of interest which compel them to sell their products as soon as they are harvested and at whatever price the buyer offers. It often happens that 60 days after harvest, when the agricultural produce has left the hands of the producer, the prices rise.

In 1962 the cost of transport was still a heavy burden on the farmer. There was still a great dearth of trained farmers and administrators.[1]

There were no new recommendations in the new plan, only a reiteration of those that had been made so often before: a better system of land tenure; the reduction of import duties on goods needed for economic development; technical aid for the improvement of agricultural methods; agricultural credits; better roads.

The two most widely-cultivated crops in Paraguay are mandioca and maize; these, with meat, are the staples of the rural diet. Little wheat is grown, but because of the increasing consumption of wheat bread in the towns, the Government has encouraged

[1] Ministerio de Agricultura y Ganadería, *Programa de 5 Años para el Mejoramiento Agrícola del Paraguay* (Asunción, 1962), pp. 4–6.

farmers to plant larger areas of this crop. When long periods of low water on the Río Paraguay interrupt the country's imports, a shortage of bread occurs.

The most important cash crop is cotton, which is now one of the principal exports.[1] Tobacco is exported to Argentina and Uruguay. Sufficient sugar-cane is grown for local needs.

Oranges grow abundantly, and at one time larger quantities of this fruit were exported to the Río de la Plata area. In recent years, however, Brazil and Argentina have overtaken Paraguay in production and marketing methods. Nevertheless, petit-grain, distilled from the leaves of the bitter-orange, is a valuable source of foreign exchange and Paraguay is still the world's largest producer of this essence, which is used as a perfume base. Petit-grain oil is extracted in a number of small distilleries in various parts of the country.[2]

Of crops yielding edible oils, cotton-seed is the most important, followed by groundnuts, which grow particularly well in Paraguay.

The Paraguayan coco palm, *mbocayá* (*Acrocomia totai Mart* or *Acrocomia sclerocarpia*), is used for many purposes. Millions of these trees grow wild in Paraguay, and they are dotted over the farmlands of the eastern region (where, incidentally, they provide a picturesque obstacle to the mechanization of agriculture). The palm, a tree of 15–25 feet in height, produces every year from three to five bunches of fruit, each bunch weighing from 5 to 10 kilos and containing up to 500 fruits the size of golf balls. Palm oil is extracted from the pulp of the fruit, coconut oil from the kernel, while the outer husk and the inner shell surrounding the kernel may be used for fuel or the extraction of certain chemicals. The residues after the extraction of oil provide cattle-feed, the leaves are useful as forage, and the tree-trunks for building. Other oil-producing crops are tung nuts and castor beans. Production of both has greatly increased in recent years.

The cultivation of coffee in the north-eastern lands around Pedro Juan Caballero has been successfully promoted by United States and Brazilian interests, and coffee is now an important export.[3]

---

[1] See App. II B, p. 85.
[2] E. Guerther, *The Essential Oils* (New York, Van Nostrand, 1948–52), vol. 3, pp. 213–27.
[3] *Cf.* App. II B, p. 85.

The *Ilex paraguariensis*, the tree that produces *yerba mate*[1] or Paraguayan tea, is native to the humid forest region where Paraguay, Argentina, and Brazil meet. Almost the entire Paraguayan and Brazilian harvest of *yerba mate* is collected from wild trees, but in Argentina there are now large plantations covering millions of acres. In the dense forests the trees grow to a great height, but under cultivation they are bushy evergreens between 12 and 30 feet high. The flavour of the wild leaf is reputed to be superior to any ever produced by cultivation. Harvest occurs between May and October (the southern winter), when the leaves are fully matured. Small branches are cut from the trees and are placed over heat to toast and dry the leaves. The branches are then threshed to remove the brittle leaves, which are finally milled.

Consumption of *yerba mate* is confined almost entirely to the Rio de la Plata countries and Brazil and Chile. The habit of drinking this infusion already existed among the Guaraníes when the Spaniards first arrived. *Yerba*, meaning 'herb', refers to the leaf of the tree. The *mate*, signifying 'gourd', is the traditional receptacle for the steeping and sipping of the beverage. With the passing of the centuries both the processed leaves and the infusion have come to be known simply as *mate*. Instead of a gourd, a coconut shell may be used, or a cow's horn, or a metal container shaped like a gourd. The *mate* has a round opening 2 or 3 inches in circumference at the top and is often elaborately decorated. A tube, made usually of silver or nickel and named a *bombilla* (Spanish for 'little pump') is inserted into the *mate*. The *bombilla* has a strainer at the lower end. Through it, the beverage is sucked.

The brewing of the drink is an art and a ritual. The *mate* is half-filled with *yerba*. A few drops of cold water are added, followed by hot water until froth appears at the opening of the *mate*. As the liquid is consumed, more water is added. The *mate* and *bombilla* are passed from hand to hand among as many persons as may be present. Each takes his sip in turn. The beverage, like coffee or tea, has a mildly stimulating effect.

Yerba mate was formerly Paraguay's principal export and main source of national wealth; but this trade has suffered from the competition of the Argentine *yerbales* and of Brazilian production.

[1] Pan American Union, *Yerba Mate* (Washington, 1946). C. A. Washburn's description of *yerba* preparation in his *History of Paraguay*, vol. 1, is a classic account of the industry.

LIVESTOCK

Soon after the founding of Asunción the Spaniards brought seven cows and a bull to Paraguy. From this nucleus, supplemented by further imports, grew herds from which a number were later transported downstream to multiply in Uruguay and Argentina. It has been estimated that the number of cattle in Paraguay in 1800 was about 3 million; but the herds were almost totally destroyed during the war of the Triple Alliance and thereafter a new beginning had to be made with animals imported from Argentina and Brazil. Paraguay now has between $5\frac{1}{2}$ and 6 million cattle, a figure which has not greatly varied in recent years. The cattle are widely owned, some on large ranches with 40,000 head or more, others on small farms. About 600,000 are slaughtered annually for domestic consumption and packing for export.[1]

The meat trade is under the control of the Corporación Paraguaya de Carnes (CORPACAR). This corporation, which is financed with both Government and private capital, has authority to fix prices and quotas for slaughtering, take censuses, and impose general regulations on the trade.

STICA, in addition to its other activities, established an experimental ranch at Estancia Barrerita in the Misiones region with 5,000 head of *criollo* cattle on land provided by the Government. The *criollo* breed, while suited to the climate, is not a great meat-producer. STICA therefore experimented with the creation of a suitable cross-bred animal, using the standard English beef cattle and the Zebu. In recent years private owners—among them Liebig's Extract of Meat Company—have also made an important contribution to cattle improvement.

Foot-and-mouth disease is endemic in Paraguay.

FORESTRY

The extent of the forest resources of the Paraguayan Chaco has never been estimated; but it is known that about half the eastern or plateau region of the republic is covered with trees. In recent years forest products have represented from 40 to 50 per cent of the value of all exports. Wood and charcoal, moreover, are the only fuels produced in the country. About two-thirds of all wood cut is used for burning.

[1] *Programa de 5 Años*, pp. 2–3.

The forests of Paraguay contain many woods that are extraordinarily resistant to decay. Charles A. Washburn wrote:

The woods are generally of a peculiar quality, and resemble nothing known in North America. The quebracho, lapacho, and urundey all grow to a size as large as the hemlock or yellow birch of New Zealand, being straight and free from limbs some fifty, sixty, or seventy feet from the ground. They are of very fine texture, and so heavy as to sink in water like iron. They are exceedingly hard to cut and work, and take a beautiful polish. But the greatest value of the wood consists in its durability. No kind of exposure seems to affect it. Sills of houses that have been exposed on one side to the sun and rain, on another to the ground, and on the other two to varying dampness and darkness, still appear to be as sound as when first put in their places, three hundred years ago. For railroad ties they must be superior to anything else known, as while larger and holding to the earth more firmly than iron, they are certainly durable enough.[1]

The tree which has been of greatest importance commercially is the quebracho ('axe-breaker') which is native to the Chaco and provides the extract used in tanning. The quantity of quebracho trees now in existence has not been estimated, but each year the cutters have to travel further in search of them and it is considered that exploitation may be unprofitable within a generation. No reafforestation has been attempted as the quebracho takes a century to grow.

The forests of eastern Paraguay cover 7·8 million hectares[2] and consist of a great variety of hardwoods. Unfortunately the most valuable species do not occur in groves, so that while there may be over 100 trees to each hectare of virgin forest, there will be only four or five of any one kind. Cedar and peterebý, the lightest of the woods exploited, are found in the central and upper Paraná districts and are in demand locally and for export. Cedar is used in building and for making furniture and plywood. Peterebý is used for furniture, doors, and window frames. Lapacho, which is cut both in the Paraná and in the upper Río Paraguay districts, is used for building.

Although the forest resources are immense, exploitation is limited by lack of roads and mechanized transport. Much of the timber has to be dragged by man or beast for long distances down forest tracks to the river bank or railway. The timber trade is

[1] *History of Paraguay*, vol. 1, pp. 435–6.
[2] FAO, *Unasylva*, vol. 2, no. 3, May–June 1948, p. 30.

almost entirely dependent on the Argentine market for exports. During times of crisis in Argentina—when the demand for timber for construction, etc., is reduced—the Paraguayan economy therefore suffers severely.

The forests are nearly all privately owned. Little has yet been done to develop a national forestry policy, but the National Agrarian Statute of 1940 made the Department of Lands and Colonization responsible for the conservation of forest resources, and legislation prohibits the exploitation of woodlands in certain areas, near villages for example, where soil erosion might follow. It is recognized that reafforestation with quick-growing trees such as eucalyptus is now necessary in the more densely populated farming region around Asunción.

Chapter IX

THE PEOPLE AND THEIR OCCUPATIONS, III

INDUSTRY

THE manufacturing industries of Paraguay are practically confined to the processing of local agricultural, pastoral, and forestry products, mainly for export, and the small-scale manufacture of consumer goods for domestic needs. Apart from a few industries such as quebracho, timber, and sugar (which are established near the source of the raw materials), and the manufacture of household goods such as pottery (produced in village workshops), most manufacturing is done in Asunción and its neighbourhood—though the principal cotton textile industry is at Pilar.

In other Latin American countries the difficulty of importing manufactured goods during the Second World War stimulated local industrial development; but in Paraguay industry was not yet sufficiently advanced to derive much benefit from the decline in foreign competition. Paraguay's canned meat had a ready market abroad during the war, but most of its industries could not develop because of the lack of machinery and spare parts; and even the traditional export industries were sometimes affected by a shortage of shipping.[1]

A representative of the Federation of British Industries who visited Paraguay in 1962 reported 'Manufacturing industry, as understood elsewhere, is negligible',[2] and a census conducted by the Paraguayan Ministry of Industry in the following year confirmed that impression: there were 5,798 manufacturing establishments and forty-seven power stations in Paraguay in 1963, but 63 per cent of these employed fewer than five workers; only 3 per cent employed more than twenty; and only 1 per cent more than fifty.[3]

Of the food-processing industries, the principal is meat—the preparation of meat for the country's urban population and of

[1] U.S. Tariff Commission, *Mining and Manufacturing Industries in Paraguay* (1946), p. 9.
[2] A. C. McKechnie, *South America's Southern Six* (London, FBI, 1963), p. 26.
[3] Bank of London & South America, *Fortnightly Review*, 25 December 1965.

canned meat and extract of meat for export. Most of the meat consumed in Paraguay is fresh. Slaughter is carried out either by the Corporación Paraguaya de Carnes in Asunción, or under the Corporation's direction elsewhere. Meat for export is processed in two foreign plants, the British-owned Liebig's Extract of Meat Company and the U.S.-owned International Products Corporation, both situated near Asunción; both companies have large holdings of land. A third concern, the Industria Paraguaya de Carnes S.A., is jointly owned by the Government and the cattle raisers.

In recent years there has been a considerable growth in the vegetable oil industry. Cotton-seed and groundnut oils are reserved by law for domestic consumption, but castor, tung, and most of the coco and palm oils are exported. The by-products of the oil-extractive industries are valuable. Cotton-seed and groundnut cake are exported, as they are not needed for feeding cattle in Paraguay, where concentrates are little used and the demand for high-quality beef-cattle is not great. The mills supply vegetable oil to the local soap industry, which produces sufficient common soap for the country's requirements, though high quality soaps are still imported. There are no facilities for the hydrogenation of oil, so no margarine is manufactured.

The manufacture of *yerba mate* is still important, as it continues to provide the traditional drink for the mass of the population, but there has been a decline in exports; production of quebracho extract suffers from the fact that the trees that remain are remote from the old factories, and severe competition now comes from other types of extract.[1] Hides and wood (the latter being shipped chiefly in the form of logs or roughly-sawn timber) are two of the chief exports; the country people grow their own tobacco, and men and women roll and smoke their own cigars—there are also several cigar and cigarette factories, but it is said that cigars rolled, at home, by a pretty girl are the best. Large quantities of *caña*, a popular rum, are distilled from sugar-cane—the distillation of alcohol is a monopoly of the Administración Paraguaya de Alcoholes, owned jointly by the State and the producers.

Limestone is plentiful in certain parts of Paraguay, and after the Second World War a cement factory was built at Valle-mí, near Concepción. There are many small factories making bricks,

[1] *Cf.* Agnes H. Hicks, *The Story of the Forestal* (London, Forestal Land, Timber & Railways Co., 1956).

mosaics, and tiles. Urban real estate being a favourite investment in Paraguay (as elsewhere), the building trade has been kept busy in recent years.

In addition to its operations in rail and river transport, domestic aviation, telecommunications, power, and the administration of public lands and forests, the State participates directly in industry through the alcohol monopoly and the Dirección de Industrias Paraguayas. This organization controls an arsenal and shipyards, and although it is intended principally to serve the needs of the armed forces it also contracts to do work for the public.

Electricity is available to about one-quarter of the population, about 80 per cent of consumers being in Asunción and its suburbs. Although the Paraná and lesser rivers offer great possibilities as sources of electric power, only a few hundred kilowatts of hydro-electric power are as yet available, and the country has relied on wood-burning thermo-electric plants. As the result of a survey, sponsored by the United States, it has now been decided to build a first hydro-electric power station on the River Acaray. This project is designed to supply electricity to Asunción and also to the upper Paraná region, where a number of land settlement programmes have been started.[1] Meanwhile imported oil is gradually replacing wood as fuel in the thermo-electric stations.

FOREIGN INVESTMENT AND FOREIGN TRADE

Traditionally the chief foreign investor in Paraguay is Argentina, with the United Kingdom second, and the United States third.

The largest Argentine investment is in quebracho, and Argentina has also substantial amounts in land, cattle, cement, milling, banking, brewing, and textiles. The major British investment was formerly the Central Railway; since the sale of the railway Britain's chief interest is in land, cattle, meat-packing, and banking. United States investments are mainly in land, cattle, meat-packing and quebracho, with smaller amounts in vegetable oils, the distribution of petroleum, and timber.

There is no formal discrimination against foreign enterprises. Indeed, recent Governments have shown themselves willing to make considerable concessions to attract foreign capital. The employment of a minimum proportion of Paraguayan nationals is

[1] See Bank of London & South America, *Fortnightly Review*, 5 September 1964 and 4 September 1965.

compulsory. In 1955 a law was promulgated granting the following guarantees and benefits to new foreign investors:

(a) exemption from customs duties on machinery, etc. imported for the purpose of establishing a new undertaking;

(b) exemption from the payment of duties on the export of new products and by-products;

(c) exemption from taxes on the formation of a new company, company contracts, etc.;

(d) a reduction of 25 per cent in business income tax;

(e) the Central Bank to provide the foreign exchange required for the remittance abroad of interest, dividends, etc., and the repatriation of capital, up to a maximum of 20 per cent of the registered capital annually;

(f) exemption (for a period not to exceed five years) from the obligation to employ the legal percentage of Paraguayan nationals.[1]

Paraguay has become a member of the Latin American Free Trade Association (LAFTA), but as yet this has had no visible effects on its trade with the other member countries (trade with Argentina, another LAFTA member, is predominant, but it has always been so), or on the progress, or lack of progress, of its manufacturing industries. The Stroessner Government's policy of strengthening the connexion with LAFTA aroused criticism at home. More than one industrial leader argued that Paraguay's industrial structure was not yet sufficiently robust to be able to sustain the rigours of participation in a free trade area. Rather paradoxically the Liberals—who might have been expected to welcome any measures that would lessen Paraguay's political and economic isolation—demanded a complete break with LAFTA, a concentration on domestic industrial development, and a return to bilateral trade agreements.[2] Meanwhile Paraguay, among LAFTA countries, was the member of whose total exports the largest percentage—on an annual average, about 30 per cent—was directed to LAFTA markets (though, in effect, this meant virtually only the one customer already referred to, Argentina).

Sidney Dell in his comprehensive study of LAFTA expresses doubt as to whether Paraguay will get its share of any benefits that the opening up of the common market may bring. He acknow-

---

[1] Board of Trade, *Economic Report*, January–February 1955, pp. 2–3.
[2] *Hispanic American Report*, November 1964.

ledges that the more prosperous Latin American nations have recognized that the least developed countries (such as Paraguay) cannot be left simply to market forces operating within a framework of regional free trade and *laissez-faire*, and that they have granted special concessions in regard to customs duties, etc., to those less-privileged countries, but, so far, the fine gestures have not been translated into concrete action. It is likely to be many years before the gap between per capita incomes in Paraguay and the more advanced LAFTA nations will have been narrowed to the point at which it can engage in unhampered free trade with them.[1]

[1] Sidney Dell, *A Latin American Common Market?* (London, OUP for RIIA, 1966), pp. 109–16.

BOLIVIA

MATO GROSSO

B R A

•Corumbá

•Tarija

P A R A G U A Y

C H A C O

Estigarribia
Filadelfia
Puerto Casado
Pedro Juan Caballero
R. Paraguay
Concepción
Horqueta
Capitán Bado
Villa Hayes
R. Pilcomayo
S. Bernardino
Asunción
Caacupé
Cnel. Oviedo Foz do Iguassú
Villarrica
R. Bermejo
R. Paraná
Formosa
Itibebuy
Borja Pte.
Stroessner
A R G E N T I N A
Pilar
S. J. Bautista
Humaitá S. Ignacio Encarnación
Corrientes Coronel Bogado
Posadas
M I S I O N E S
B R A Z I L

R. Uruguay

R. Paraná

U R U G U A Y

Buenos Aires
Río de la Plata
•Montevideo

PARAGUAY
POLITICAL AND
COMMUNICATIONS

——— *Roads*

++++++ *Railways*

0   MILES   200

Chapter X

COMMUNICATIONS

UNTIL the coming of the aeroplane the only practicable routes from Asunción to the outside world were by river or rail to Buenos Aires, and even today the bulk of the traffic follows that same course. The main waters of the Paraná and Paraguay rivers were internationalized after the War of the Triple Alliance, but the country's life-line is still at the mercy of Argentina, as it was at the time of Rosas. Furthermore, Argentina's big share in the carrying of Paraguayan imports and exports, though no longer a complete monopoly, still indicates that the economy of the upstream republic is far from secure. The delays and expense of river transport place Paraguay at a disadvantage in foreign markets.

Paraguay has a little over 300 miles of public railways and some 420 miles of private industrial tracks. The one main line in the country, the Ferrocarril Central, 274 miles long, runs from Asunción through Villarrica to Encarnación. Its history[1] dates back to 1854 when Carlos Antonio López engaged two English engineers named Valpy and Burrell to make surveys for a line between Asunción and the town of Paraguarí. Construction was started immediately under the direction of the two engineers with three battalions of infantry as labour, and the railway is thus one of the oldest in the continent. The first section of 45 miles to Trinidad was inaugurated in 1861, but the War of the Triple Alliance prevented further work and the extension to Villarrica (90 miles from Asunción) could not be completed until 1886. The State then sold the line to a British firm on the condition that the line be continued to Encarnación on the Alto Paraná river. The subsequent story of the railway is beset with financial disappointments. The line did not reach Encarnación until 1911, the gauge having been changed meanwhile from 5 ft 6 in. to 4 ft 8½ in. so as to conform to the adjacent Argentine railway system. In 1913–14 the railway-

[1] The following account is based on a memorandum by A. G. Cooper preserved at the offices of the Paraguayan Central Railway Company in London.

ferry service across the Paraná to the Argentine river port of Posadas was created, completing the railway link between Asunción and Buenos Aires, a total distance of 938 miles.

A branch line was built from Borja (a junction south of Villarrica) to Abaí, a settlement forty miles east of the main line and on the edge of the great forest area. It was proposed that this line should be extended to Foz do Iguassú on the Alto Paraná, thus providing a railway connexion with Brazil.

In recent decades the Ferrocarril Central has suffered increasingly from road competition; the principal new roads were not 'feeders' to the railway but were trunk routes from Asunción that passed through the central region of eastern Paraguay and to some extent duplicated the railway service. For many years the company paid no interest or dividends. Most of the equipment needed renewal. Finally in 1959 the British board of directors announced that the company could not continue incurring losses, so the Paraguayan Government assumed responsibility for operating the railway, which was purchased by the State two years later.

The only other common carrier railway is the State-owned Ferrocarril Nacional Norte of about thirty-five miles running inland from the river port of Concepción to Horqueta. It is a metregauge logging-type railway with primitive rolling stock. The line was planned in 1919, with the agreement of Brazil, to run eastwards as far as Pedro Juan Caballero, where it would connect with the Brazilian railway system. Its chief use at present is as a goods line serving the logging camps and stock-raising area east of Concepción.

In addition there are some half a dozen narrow-gauge lines running inland from the smaller ports on the Upper Paraguay. All but one run westwards into the Chaco and serve the quebracho industry. The longest of the lines, with a total length of 223 miles, penetrates over 100 miles westwards from Puerto Casado. This railway, in addition to its use as an industrial line, is an important means of access to the western Chaco. It provides communications for the Mennonite colony, and was one of the chief supply routes during the Chaco War. Roads were built by the army westwards from its terminus towards the Bolivian frontier.

Paraguay still lacks a network of modern highways. Most of the roads in the interior are little more than earth tracks, suitable only for ox-carts, which are the chief means of transport in rural districts. During heavy rainstorms these roads become impassable.

Successive governments, however, have recognized the need for improving internal land transportation and river shipping facilities. A comprehensive road plan was drawn up in the late 1930s and with United States assistance, the construction of two major trunk roads was begun. The first of these two highways to be built was Route II—the Ruta Mariscal Estigarribia—which runs eastwards from Asunción for about 115 miles to Villarrica, via the popular hillside resort of Caacupé and the town of Coronel Oviedo (whence an extension now continues to the banks of the Alto Paraná). The second highway was Route I, which was planned to run southwards from Asunción, through the Misiones, to Encarnación. Additions were made, from time to time, to these roads, but it was not until the assumption of the presidency by General Stroessner in the 1950s that the next real impetus was given to road-building. President Stroessner extended a branch of Route II from Coronel Oviedo to the small river port that was re-named Puerto Presidente Stroessner (formerly Puerto Presidente Franco) on the Alto Paraná, whence a new international bridge, crossing the river, now joins Paraguay to Brazil. Stroessner inaugurated another road that had long been dreamed of and talked about, the trans-Chaco highway from Villa Hayes to the frontier of Bolivia; and he reached an agreement with Argentina for the building of a bridge across the Río Paraguay to link the suburbs of Asunción with the north Argentine road system, replacing the present ferry.

Omnibuses now ply on the highways between the more prosperous towns and villages of Paraguay's central region, while the old railway languishes.

Nevertheless, Paraguay is still essentially a riverside nation, so that plans for modernizing the ports, dredging the rivers, and adding to the country's fleet of river-boats are at least as important for the national economy as plans for the improvement of roads and road transport. Most of the goods exported and imported by Paraguay are conveyed by river. As modern ocean-going ships cannot reach upstream Asunción,[1] goods coming and going be-

[1] In 1953 the Compañía Marítima Holandesa began monthly direct sailings between Europe and Asunción, using two ships of 800 tons deadweight; and Lamport and Holt Line inaugurated a similar service between Liverpool and Asunción.

tween the more distant countries have to be transhipped into shallower vessels at Buenos Aires or Montevideo. This of course causes delay and additional expense; in fact freights from Buenos Aires to Asunción have at times been higher than on the same goods between England and Buenos Aires. During most of the year the Paraná–Paraguay waterway is navigable for boats of 12-foot draught to Asunción and for 6-foot draught vessels as far as Corumbá. In the season of low water, from January to May, the larger boats cannot reach Asunción and goods frequently have to be transhipped at the Argentine port of Corrientes. The main channel of the Paraná follows a winding and inconstant course, and, in spite of the experience and vigilance of the river pilots, steamers not infrequently become lodged for a while in newly-formed sandbanks. During low water the cargo to be carried is often reduced to one-third of the normal amount, and the river transport companies impose a low-water surcharge. The Upper Paraná is usually navigable by 6-foot draught vessels as far as Encarnación.

Periodically the entrance to the port of Asunción, through which most of Paraguay's foreign trade passes, becomes silted up; and the equipment of the port is quite inadequate for present-day requirements; plans for modernizing the port and reconstructing the whole of the surrounding area have been approved.[1]

After the War of the Triple Alliance, Paraguay became excessively dependent on Argentine shipping for carrying on her river traffic. In colonial times the Paraguayans were well known as ship-builders. Under the two López the shipyard outside Asunción was quite well equipped, vessels were also purchased in Europe, and at the outbreak of the War of the Triple Alliance Paraguay had a merchant fleet of river and ocean-going ships. These were converted for war use and all were lost during hostilities. In 1945 the Government began the creation of a new State merchant fleet, but ten years later it was estimated that as much as 90 per cent of the goods traffic between Asunción and Buenos Aires was still carried in Argentine vessels—and of course it was the Argentines who fixed the charges. President Stroessner reduced dependence on Argentine river transport to some extent by ordering ships for the Paraguayan river fleet from Spain and Japan; some critics of

[1] The London firm of architects acting as consultants for this scheme announced, early in 1966, that it would take twenty years to complete. *Financial Times*, 22 February 1966.

his programme maintained that the ships that he ordered were too big and that barges would have served Paraguay's needs better.

Jet aircraft from many of the chief international lines provide regular services to Asunción. For the use of local aeroplanes, most of the provincial towns and larger estancias have earth or grass air-strips.

CONCLUSION: A SORT OF ARCADIA

'. . . *often in Paraguay there hangs over the landscape that air of magic noted by so many travellers, as though one had infiltrated into the enchanted country of one's childhood romance-reading, a sort of Shangri-la, a province sealed off from the rest of the world'.*

'*It might be objected that a country under a Dictator is ipso facto disqualified from enthusiastic claims of travellers that it is any sort of Arcadia. . . . [We do not mean] that the evident happiness of the Paraguayan nation—as a whole—is justification of their form of government; the Paraguayans have a deeper secret: that of being happy regardless. And in that is there not something of that felicity traditionally associated with the Arcadia of literature?*'

GORDON MEYER, 'The River and the People', 1965.

PARAGUAY grew up in isolation, with its own language, legends, and customs. Because of its remoteness, communication with the outside world was always difficult and slow; and the isolation was aggravated by events. As has been shown, after the emancipation from Spain all international communication was prevented for long periods by the action of the nation's rulers and surrounding States. In a single century the Paraguayan people endured the 'closed door' of Dr Francia's dictatorship, the blockade of the river by the Buenos Aires autocrat Rosas, the rigid frontier control imposed by Solano López during the War of the Triple Alliance, and the enemy's ever narrower encirclement. Even since López's death the country has been virtually inaccessible for months at a time when, as the result of internal conflict, normal traffic has been interrupted—or simply because the low level of the Río Paraguay has prevented river-steamers from completing their journeys.

Isolation is natural to this land and its people, and although the lack of easy and regular communication with other regions has undoubtedly retarded economic and social development on modern Western lines, it has also been the direct cause of the persistence of the homogeneity in the race and the remarkably strong national character, both of which are highly valued by Paraguayans. It can even be argued that Paraguay has been more often weakened than strengthened by the opening of its frontiers. Wars, waged by this nation in isolation and against formidable opponents, have not destroyed it. But a serious threat of disintegration occurs when the door is open, for, as already explained, it is then that the rebels return home. Paraguay can derive economic benefit from the influx of foreign capital and technicians, but must protect itself against the draining away of human and material resources—the emigration of workers, who seek higher wages in the neighbouring States, and of students, writers, musicians, who wish to participate in the wider culture of the larger cities; the smuggling of cattle out of the country, for the higher prices that they fetch in Brazil; the exporting of financial assets.

The tragedy of this natural Arcadia, therefore, is that it can neither live in idyllic solitude nor compete on equal terms with the great nations that surround it. The predicament recurs in every branch of life. Paraguayan literature, for example, has been gravely weakened by the fact that any writer who wishes to appeal to a public that is not merely parochial, must write in the Spanish language. The most authentic and successful Paraguayan literature—such as the poems and plays of Julio Correa (b. 1908) and some of the poetry of Manuel Ortiz Guerrero (1897–1933)[1]—is in Guaraní, which is the language in which the people naturally express their emotions. 'The Paraguayans love, hate, and fight in Guaraní. In this tongue they shout on the football fields and whisper their declarations of love in the dark corners of the patios of their old colonial houses.'[2] It is a rich language wherein a single word often combines both a noun and its attendant adjective, the subject and its quality. *Pyjharé* means not only 'night' but also 'infinity'; *purajhei* signifies simultaneously 'song' and 'the manner of uttering pretty things'; and *cuña* has the combined meaning of 'women' and 'Devil's tongue'.[3]

It has been remarked that 'Even the educated Paraguayan abandons restraint the moment he talks Guaraní', and a recent traveller has noted that Rogelio Espinoza (a distinguished Paraguayan landowner, with an English wife) is grave, when speaking in Spanish, but 'joking, mischievous, even unpredictable' when he changes to Guaraní.[4]

---

[1] Ortiz Guerrero died of leprosy.
[2] Walter Wey, *La Poesía Paraguaya*; *Historia de una Incógnita* (Montevideo, Biblioteca Alfar, 1951), p. 24.
[3] ibid. p. 104.   [4] Meyer, *The River and the People*, p. 168.

Paraguay does not lack poets, and if none of them has yet attained international fame it is, perhaps, because, as Augusto Roa Bastos (b. 1918), himself one of the most talented of younger Paraguayan writers, has remarked,

the Spanish version of their ideas and sentiments is a translation and therefore a betrayal. When they write poetry in Spanish they feel constrained, and their creative power is weakened. . . . The same is true of prose fiction. Paraguay really has no novelists in Spanish, although Guaraní folk-lore abounds in long narratives and stories. The explanation is doubtless that the Spanish language is inappropriate for expressing dialogue which was originally conceived in Guaraní.[1]

Paraguayan literature may be split by bilingualism, but the popular music of the country is whole, and eloquent: the languid *guaranías* composed by Asunción Flores and the lilting polkas—played on harp and guitar—do convey something of the spirit of the people to foreign audiences.

Dr and Mrs Service, authors of the book *Tobatí*, maintain that no such thing as 'Guaraní culture' exists in Paraguay, merely a form of lower-class Hispanic culture—though they have to concede, of course, that Guaraní is the real language and that Spanish is 'more or less artificially grafted on'.[2]

But then the Services are utterly pessimistic about this isolated, agricultural nation:

The internal market for agricultural produce is very small, as there are no large cities and the percentage of non-agricultural population is the smallest in [the western] hemisphere, except for Haiti. The foreign market is almost non-existent, partly because the only egress is via the Argentine-dominated Paraguay River, where shipping costs are enormous. The cycle of sale of crops for cash, in order to invest in equipment or more land, in order to increase production for more profit, never received the necessary impetus to get it started and never can, until a sufficient market exists. . . . Piecemeal economic aid of the sort offered by loans and technical assistance programs sponsored by the United States of America may lead to improvements in parts of the economy or at least may benefit certain individuals. . . . But the nation itself does not have the means to maintain the improvements now initiated, much less to continue further development. . . . The agrarian bulk of the population in Paraguay will remain peasants until their produce can be sold in the external market or internally to a larger proportion of non-agriculturalists who are producing something else for the external market.[3]

---

[1] These quotations are from a letter from Augusto Roa Bastos to the author.
[2] E. R. and H. S. Service, *Tobatí*, p. 147.   [3] ibid. pp. 295–7.

Conclusion: A Sort of Arcadia

Meanwhile, although Paraguay is not quite the paradise that it might have been, it is a land of character and great charm where every man can grow enough food for his own family and sing his melodious Guaraní songs to his heart's content, without a thought for the Services' pronouncement that they are not Guaraní at all.

APPENDIX

I. POPULATION[1]

A. Growth of Population, 1865–1962

1865	525,000
1871	221,000*
1900	490,000
1936	931,000
1940	1,014,800
1942	1,071,700
1950	1,405,600†
1962	1,816,890†

* End of the War of the Triple Alliance.
† Census.

B. Census of 1962

Total Population	1,816,890
Men	895,551
Women	921,339

Principal Towns:

Asunción	305,160*
Villarrica†	30,998
Coronel Oviedo	44,565
Encarnación	35,781
Concepción	33,282

* About 450,000 including surrounding districts.
† Still considered the second town in Paraguay, although no longer the second largest.

Average Density of Population
Eastern Paraguay 28 inhabitants per sq. m.
The Chaco 2 ,, ,, ,, ,,

[1] Dirección General de Estadística y Censos (mimeographed sheets, undated).

II. FOREIGN TRADE[1]

A. BALANCE OF TRADE

(U.S. $ million)

	Exports	*Imports*	*Balance*
1953	30·66	24·31	+ 6·35
1954	33·97	32·88	+ 1·09
1955	35·10	28·96	+ 6·14
1956	36·69	24·63	+12·06
1957	32·90	27·36	+ 5·54
1958	34·10	32·59	+ 1·51
1959	31·20	26·19	+ 5·01
1960	26·98	32·46	− 5·48
1961	30·68	34·73	− 4·05
1962	33·47	34·26	− 0·79
1963	40·19	32·60	+ 7·59
1964	49·77	33·77	+16·00
1965	57·2	44·0	+13·2

[1] SOURCE: for all tables in App. II; Bank of London & S. America *Fortnightly Review* (various issues).

B. EXPORTS

PRINCIPAL COMMODITIES

(U.S. $ million)

	1962	*1963*	*1964*
Meat products	7·47	10·52	14·75
Wood	6·66	4·74	7·15
Cotton fibres	2·47	3·20	4·20
Oilseeds	2·33	4·43	3·98
Quebracho extract	2·53	2·81	3·98
Tobacco	3·09	3·16	3·74
Coffee	2·84	3·31	3·18
Essential oils	1·08	1·28	1·46
Yerba mate	0·92	0·88	1·35

DIRECTION OF EXPORT TRADE

(*U.S. $ million*)

	1962	*1963*	*1964*
Areas:			
Latin America	11·10	10·70	15·20
Western Europe	9·33	12·68	13·87
North America (U.S.A. & Canada)	7·09	9·32	12·00
Principal countries:			
U.S.A. (meat products & oilseeds)	6·97	9·06	11·81
Argentina (wood, cotton fibres, & oilseeds)	9·61	8·60	11·64
U.K. (meat products)	3·47	4·54	6·68

C. IMPORTS

PRINCIPAL COMMODITIES

(*U.S. $ million*)

	1962	*1963*	*1964*
Machinery, apparatus	5·46	4·06	4·93
Wheat & products	5·32	4·92	4·77
Vehicles	5·05	3·76	4·64
Fuels & lubricants	3·54	4·01	4·15
Iron, steel, & manufactures	1·63	1·54	2·04

DIRECTION OF IMPORT TRADE

(*U.S. $ million*)

	1962	*1963*	*1964*
Areas:			
Western Europe	10·81	8·84	10·80
Latin America	6·10	8·65	10·30
North America (U.S.A. & Canada)	10·80	9·72	7·80
Principal Countries:			
Argentina (wheat & products, & fuels & lubricants)	5·03	7·56	9·44
U.S.A. (wheat, machinery, & vehicles)	10·77	9·57	7·19
W. Germany (machinery & vehicles)	4·72	3·42	4·44
U.K. (vehicles)	2·58	2·53	2·30
Netherlands Antilles (fuels & lubricants)	2·35	2·34	2·09

III. United Kingdom Trade with Paraguay

A. Balance of Trade
(£ million)

	U.K. exports and re-exports	U.K. imports	Balance
1953	1·16	0·72	+0·44
1954	1·25	1·17	+0·08
1955	0·66	1·05	−0·39
1956	0·61	1·92	−1·31
1957	1·16	2·39	−1·24
1958	0·76	1·41	−0·65
1959	0·87	1·76	−0·89
1960	0·83	1·84	−1·01
1961	0·99	2·30	−1·30
1962	1·11	2·31	−1·20
1963	0·82	2·03	−1·21
1964	0·95	2·31	−1·36

[1] Source: As App. II.

B. Commodity Composition, 1964 (Principal Items)

£'000

U.K. Exports

Beverages (chiefly whisky) & tobacco	126
Iron & steel	183
Machinery	130
Transport equipment	139

U.K. Imports

Meat (in airtight containers; meat extracts & essences) 1,943

Source: As App. II.

IV. AGRICULTURAL PRODUCTION 1964–5

	Area sown ('ooo ha.)	Production ('ooo tons)
Alfalfa	5·0	18·0
Beans	31·5	23·6
Castor seed	9·7	12·1
Cotton	56·8	42·0
Maize	161·5	210·0
Manioc, mandioca	108·0	1,512·0
Onions	3·0	14·1
Peanuts	22·6	19·2
Potatoes, incl. sweet potatoes	12·6	108·1
Rice	8·0	21·6
Soya beans	11·3	18·0
Sugar-cane	26·8	991·6
Tobacco	13·6	17·0
Wheat	9·0	8·0

SOURCE: As App. II.

BIBLIOGRAPHY

I. GENERAL

Brady, George S. *The Railways of South America*, pt II. U.S. Dept. of Commerce, 1927.

Davies, Howell, ed. *The South American Handbook*. London, Trade & Travel Publications. (Published annually. Contains useful information for travellers.)

Dell, Sidney. *A Latin American Common Market?* London, Oxford University Press for Royal Institute of International Affairs, 1966.

García Calderón, F. *Latin America: its Rise and Progress*, trs. Bernard Miall. 7th ed. Fisher Unwin, 1924. (First published 1913.)

Gordon, Wendell C. *The Economy of Latin America*. New York, Columbia University Press, 1950.

Hanson, Simon G. *Economic Development in Latin America*. Washington, Inter-American Affairs Press, 1951.

Haring, C. H. *The Spanish Empire in America*. New York, Oxford University Press, 1947.

Hughlett, Lloyd J., ed. *Industrialization in Latin America*. New York, McGraw-Hill, 1946.

Humphreys, R. A. *British Consular Reports on the Trade and Politics of Latin America, 1824–26*. London, Royal Historical Society, 1940. (Camden 3rd ser., vol. 63.)

—— *Latin American History: a Guide to the Literature in English*. London, Oxford University Press for Royal Institute of International Affairs, 1958.

James, Preston E. *Latin America*. London, Cassell, 1943. 3rd ed. New York, Odyssey Press, 1959.

Jane, Cecil. *Liberty and Despotism in Spanish America*. Oxford, Clarendon Press, 1929.

Joslin, David. *A Century of Banking in Latin America*. London, Oxford University Press, 1963. (Reference to the first establishment of a British bank in Asunción.)

Kirkpatrick, F. A. *Latin America: a Brief History*. Cambridge University Press, 1938.

Macdonald, Austin F. *Latin American Politics and Government*. New York, Crowell, 1949.

Mulhall, Michael G. *The English in South America*. Buenos Aires, 'The Standard', 1878.

Peterson, Harold F. *Argentina and the United States, 1810–1960*. State University of New York, 1964. (Many references to Paraguay.)

Rippy, J. Fred. *Historical Evolution of Latin America*. 3rd ed. New York, Crofts, 1945.

—— *Latin America and the Industrial Age*. New York, Putnam, 1944.

Steward, Julian H., ed. *Handbook of South American Indians*. 6 vols. Washington, Smithsonian Institution, Bureau of American Ethnology, Bulletin 143, 1949.

II. PARAGUAYAN HISTORY, POLITICS, AND SOCIAL CONDITIONS

Acosta, César. 'La Población Rural del Paraguay', in Unión Panamericana, Departmento de Asuntos Culturales, *Materiales para el Estudio de la Clase Media en la América Latina*, vol. 3. Washington, 1950.

Alexander, Robert J. *The Bolivian National Revolution*. Rutgers University Press, 1958. (The Chaco War is seen from the Bolivian angle.)

89

Bibliography

Artaza, Policarpo. *Ayala, Estigarribia y el Partido Liberal.* 2nd ed. Buenos Aires, Ayacucho, 1946. (A partisan interpretation of Paraguayan politics by an exiled Liberal newspaper-owner.)

Báez, Cecilio. *Ensayo sobre el Doctor Francia y la Dictadura en Sud-América.* Asunción, 1910.

—— *Historia Diplomática del Paraguay.* 2 vols. Asunción, Imprenta Nacional, 1931–2.

—— *Resumen de la Historia del Paraguay desde la Epoca de la Conquista hasta el Año 1880.* Asunción, Kraus, 1910. (Báez was a distinguished Liberal teacher and statesman.)

Benítez, Justo Pastor, *Carlos Antonio López.* Buenos Aires, Ayacucho, 1949.

—— *Estigarribia, el Soldado del Chaco.* Buenos Aires, Difusam, 1943.

—— *Formación Social del Paraguay.* Asunción and Buenos Aires, Editorial América-Sapucai, 1955.

—— *El Solar Guaraní.* Buenos Aires, Ayacucho, 1947.

Bourgade la Dardye, E. de. *Paraguay: the land and the people, natural wealth and commercial capabilities.* London, Philip, 1892.

Box, Pelham Horton. *The Origins of the Paraguayan War.* 2 vols. Urbana, Illinois, 1929. University of Illinois, Studies in the Social Sciences, xv, nos. 3 and 4. (The standard work on the origins of the War of the Triple Alliance.)

Boxer, C. R. *Salvador de Sá and the Struggle for Brazil and Angola, 1602–86.* University of London, Athlone Press, 1952.

Bray, Arturo. *Hombres y Epocas del Paraguay.* Buenos Aires, Editorial Difusam, 1943. (Studies of Francia, Carlos Antonio López, Francisco Solano López, Caballero, Eligio Ayala, and others.)

Cardozo, Efraím. 'Paraguay Independiente', in A. Ballesteros, ed., *Historia de América*, vol. 21. Barcelona, Salvat 1949.

Charlevoix, P. F. X. de. *Histoire du Paraguay.* 3 vols. Paris, 1756. Eng. trs.: *The History of Paraguay.* 2 vols. Dublin, 1769. (The famous history of the Jesuit missions by a Jesuit Father who never went to Paraguay.)

Chaves, Julio C. *El Supremo Dictador: Biografía de José Gaspar de Francia.* Buenos Aires, Difusam, 1942.

Decoud, José Segundo. *History of Paraguay.* Washington, USGPO, 1902.

Fretz, Joseph Winfield. *Pilgrims in Paraguay.* Scottdale, Mennonite Publishing House, 1953. (The story of Mennonite colonization in Latin America, with special reference to Paraguay.)

Gandía, Enrique de. *Historia del Gran Chaco.* Buenos Aires, Roldán, 1929.

Garay, Blas. *Tres Ensayos sobre Historia del Paraguay.* Asunción, Guarania, 1942.

Gelly, Juan Andrés. *El Paraguay: Lo que fué, lo ques es, y lo que será.* Paris, Editorial las Indias, 1926.

González, J. Natalicio. *Geografía del Paraguay.* Mexico, Guarania, 1964.

Graham, R. B. Cunninghame. *Portrait of a Dictator: Francisco Solano López (Paraguay, 1865–70).* London, Heinemann, 1933. (A very readable denunciation of López which is banned in Paraguay.)

—— *A Vanished Arcadia.* London, Heinemann, 1901.

Grahame, Stewart. *Where Socialism Failed.* London, Murray, 1912. (A biased account of the Australian colonies in Paraguay.)

Herrera, Luis Alberto de. *La Diplomacia Oriental en el Paraguay.* 5 vols. Montevideo, Barrevio y Ramos, 1908–26.

Ibarra, Alonso. *Las Revoluciones Paraguayas en Letras de Molde (1870–1949).* Asunción, Popular, 1949.

Instituto Histórico y Geográfico del Uruguay. *Artigas: Homenaje en el Centenario de su Muerte.* Montevideo, Imprenta Nacional, 1952. Cursos de Conferencias, Año 1950. (Contains lectures on Artigas's relations with Paraguay by Carlos Pastore, Julio César Chaves, Juan Stefanich, and R. Antonio Ramos.)

Bibliography

—— *El Paraguayo Independiente*. Asunción, *1850*. Prologue by Carlos Pastore. Montevideo, 1950. (*El Paraguayo Independiente*, founded in 1845, was Paraguay's first newspaper. It was published weekly by the Government, its original purpose being to counter the aggressive propaganda of the Argentine dictator, Rosas. In 1852 this newspaper was renamed *El Semanario*. It was the official organ of Solano López before and during the War of the Triple Alliance.)

Jover Peralta, A. *El Guaraní en la Geografía de América*. Buenos Aires, Tupá, 1950.

Koebel, W. H. *Paraguay*. London, Fisher Unwin, 1917.

Krause, Annemarie Elizabeth. *Mennonite Settlement in the Paraguayan Chaco*. University of Chicago, Department of History (Research Paper 25), 1952.

Livermore, H. V. 'New Australia', in *Hispanic American Historical Review*, August 1950, pp. 290–313. (The Australian colony in Paraguay.)

Lugon, C. *La République Communiste Chrétienne des Guaranis, 1610–1768*. Paris, Éditions Ouvrières Économie et Humanisme, 1949.

Maldonado, Silvio. *El Paraguay*. México, Fondo de Cultura Económica, 1952. (Colección Tierra Firme; the section dealing with agrarian reform is particularly useful.)

Ministerio de Economía. *Las Colonias Mennonitas en el Chaco Paraguayo*. Asunción, 1934.

Mörner, Magnus, *The Political and Economic Activities of the Jesuits in the La Plata Region: the Hapsburg Era*. Trs. by Albert Read, Stockholm, Library and Institute of Ibero-American Studies, 1953.

Pastore, Carlos. *La Lucha por la Tierra en el Paraguay: Proceso histórico y legislativo*. Montevideo, Antequera, 1949.

Pendle, George. 'Eliza Lynch and the English in Paraguay, 1853–1875', in *History Today*, May 1954, pp. 346–53.

Peterson, Harold F. 'Edward A. Hopkins: a Pioneer Promoter in Paraguay', in *Hispanic American Historical Review*, May 1942, pp. 245–61.

Pérez Acosta, Juan F. *Migraciones Históricas del Paraguay a la Argentina*. Buenos Aires, Talleres Gráficos Optimus, 1952.

Pitaud, Henri. *Paraguay, Terre vierge*. Paris, Chambriand, 1950.

Poucel. *Le Paraguay Moderne*. . . . Marseilles, Marius Olive, 1867.

Prieto, Justo. *Paraguay, la Provincia Gigante de las Indias*. Buenos Aires, 1951.

Raine, Philip. *Paraguay*. New Brunswick, N.J., Scarecrow Press, 1956. (A reliable general account.)

Reh, Emma, *Paraguayan Rural Life: Survey of Food Problems, 1943–5*. Washington, Institute of Inter-American Affairs (Foods Supply Division), 1946. (An excellent account of rural living conditions.)

Ronde, Philip de. *Paraguay: a Gallant Little Nation*. New York, Putnam, 1935.

Sánchez, Luis Alberto. *Reportaje al Paraguay*. Asunción, Guarania, 1949.

Sánchez Quell, H. *Estructura y Función del Paraguay Colonial*. Buenos Aires, 1947.

—— *Política Internacional del Paraguay*. 2nd ed. Buenos Aires, Tupá. 1945.

Service, Elman R. and Helen S. *Tobatí: Paraguayan Town*. University of Chicago Press, 1954. (A detailed study of life in a representative rural town.)

Stefanich, Juan. *Artigas, Francia y el Paraguay, el Ostracismo del Prócer Oriental en Tierra Paraguaya y Orígenes del Derecho de Asilo en América*. Montevideo, Tipografía Mercantil, 1950.

—— *El Paraguay Nuevo*. Buenos Aires, Claridad, 1943. (The apologia of the movement headed by Colonel Rafael Franco.)

Vargas Peña, Benjamín. *Los Ideales del Paraguay*. Corrientes (Argentina), Editorial Corrientes, 1954. (Political essays by a Paraguayan Liberal refugee.)

War in the River Plate in 1865. London, Hardwicke, 1865.

Warren, Carlos A. *Emancipación Económica Americana*, vol. 18: *Paraguay*. Montevideo, Ceibo, 1946. (An apologia of the Morínigo régime.)

Warren, Harris Gaylord. *Paraguay: an Informal History*. University of Oklahoma Press, 1949. (The most comprehensive modern book on Paraguay.)

Bibliography

Ynsfrán, Pablo Max, ed. *The Epic of the Chaco: Marshal Estigarribia's Memoirs of the Chaco War, 1932–5.* Austin, University of Texas Press, 1950. (Latin American Studies, VIII; the most important book on the Chaco War.)

—— *La Expedición Norteamericana contra el Paraguay, 1858–1859. Primera Parte: Los Antecedentes.* Mexico–Buenos Aires, 1954.

—— 'Sam Ward's Bargain with President López of Paraguay', in *Hispanic American Historical Review*, August 1954, pp. 313–31. (The sequel to the quarrel of President Carlos Antonio López with the United States.)

Zinny, Antonio. *Historia de los Gobernantes del Paraguay, 1535–1887.* Buenos Aires, Imprenta de Mayo, 1887.

III. Travel and Description

Azara, Félix de. *Voyages dans l'Amérique Méridionale, depuis 1781 jusqu'en 1801...* 4 vols. and atlas. Paris, 1809.

Bossi, Bartolomé. *Viage Pintoresco por los Rios Paraná, Paraguay,* etc. Paris, Dupray de la Mahérie, 1865.

Bougainville, Louis de. *Voyage autour du Monde...* Paris, 1771.

Burton, Richard F. *Letters from the Battlefields of Paraguay.* London, 1870.

Craig, C. W. Thurlow. *Paraguayan Interlude.* London, Barker, 1935.

Davie, John Constanse. *Letters from Paraguay.* London, Robinson, 1805.

Dobrizhoffer, Martin. *An Account of the Abipones, an Equestrian People of Paraguay.* 3 vols. London, Murray, 1822. (Originally published in Latin at Vienna in 1784).

Durrell, Gerald. *The Drunken Forest.* London, Hart-Davis, 1956. (Travel, mostly in the Chaco.)

Gibson, Sir Christopher. *Enchanted Trails.* London, Museum Press, 1948.

Graty, Alfred M. du. *La République du Paraguay.* Brussels, Muquardt, 1862. (Contains the best illustrations in existence of the town of Asunción in the time of Carlos Antonio López.)

Grubb, W. Barbrooke. *A Church in the Wilds.* London, Seeley, 1914.

—— *Among the Indians of the Paraguayan Chaco.* London, South American Missionary Society, 1904.

—— *An Unknown People in an Unknown Land.* London, Seeley, 1911.

Hills, J. W. and Ianthe Dunbar. *The Golden River. Sport and Travel in Paraguay.* London, Philip Allan, 1922.

Hunt, R. J. *The Livingstone of South America; the Life and Adventures of W. Barbrooke Grubb....* London, Seeley, 1933.

Hutchinson, Thomas J. *The Parana; with Incidents of the Paraguayan War, and South American Recollections.* London, Stanford, 1868.

Jones, Tom B. *South America Rediscovered.* University of Minnesota Press, 1949.

Kennedy, A. J. *La Plata, Brazil, and Paraguay, during the Present War.* London, Stanford, 1869.

Knight, E. F. *The Cruise of the 'Falcon'.* 2 vols, London, Sampson Low, 1884. (One of the best of the up-river travel books.)

Koebel, W. H. *In Jesuit Land.* London, Stanley Paul, 1906.

Land of Lace and Legend: an Informal Guide to Paraguay. 2nd ed. Asunción, La Cólmena, 1960. (A popular guide-book.)

Macdonald, Alexander K. *Picturesque Paraguay.* London, Kelley, 1911.

Mansfield, C. B. *Paraguay, Brazil, and the Plate: Letters written in 1852–3.* Cambridge, Macmillan, 1856.

Masterman, George Frederick. *Seven Eventful Years in Paraguay.* London, Low, 1869.

Meyer, Gordon. *The River and the People.* London, Methuen, 1965. (A perceptive travel book.)

Bibliography

Page, Thomas Jefferson. *La Plata, the Argentine Confederation and Paraguay.* London, Trubner, 1859.

Parish, Sir Woodbine, *Buenos Aires and the Provinces of the Rio de la Plata.* London, Murray, 1838.

Pitaud, Henri. *Les Français au Paraguay.* Bordeaux and Paris, Editions Bière, 1955.

Powell, David, 'The Republic of Paraguay' in Francis Galton, ed., *Vacation Tourists and Notes of Travel, 1862–3.* London, Macmillan, 1864.

Rengger, J. R. and M. Longchamp. *Essai Historique sur la Révolution du Paraguay, et le Gouvernement Dictatorial du Docteur Francia.* Paris, Hector Bossange, 1827.

Robertson, J. P. and W. P. *Letters on Paraguay.* 3 vols. London, Murray, 1838–9.

Smith, Willard H. and Verna Graber. *Paraguayan Interlude.* Scottdale, Pennsylvania, Herald Press, 1950.

Thompson, George. *The War in Paraguay, with a Historical Sketch of the Country and its People.* London, Longmans, 1869.

Thompson, R. W. *Land of Tomorrow. A Story of South America.* London, Duckworth, 1936.

—— *Voice from the Wilderness.* London, Faber, 1940. (This book was republished in 1942 with the title *Germans and Japs in South America.* A revised edition, with the original title, was published by Macdonald in 1947.)

Washburn, Charles A. *The History of Paraguay.* 2 vols. Boston, Lee & Shepard, 1871.

IV. LITERATURE

Baillie, Alexander F. *A Paraguayan Treasure: the Search and the Discovery.* London, Simpkin, Marshall, 1887. (A novel concerning the treasure that Solano López is supposed to have buried at some unknown place during the War of the Triple Alliance. In an undated autograph letter which is pasted in the copy of this book in the Canning House Library, Baillie wrote: '*A Paraguayan Treasure* is founded on fact. There is, I believe, no doubt that a considerable treasure was buried, and it is perfectly true that a number of people were shot, in order that the secret of the spot where it was hidden might not be divulged. Many attempts have been made to discover it, and Mrs Lynch saw me herself on the subject, and wanted me to buy the secret, but as a matter of fact it has never been discovered, and the latter part of the book is fictitious.' Attempts to discover the treasure are still made from time to time. In 1943 a party of Paraguayans, whose leader had a new clue to its whereabouts, unsuccessfully dug a deep pit in the red earth in the garden of the British Legation at Asunción.)

Barrett, William E. *Woman on Horseback.* London, Davies, 1938. (A novel about Mme Lynch.)

Bilbao, M. *Elisa Linch [sic] Juicio Crítico dado por el Diario la Republica.* Buenos Aires, 1870.

Blomberg, Héctor Pedro. *La Dama del Paraguay.* Buenos Aires, Editora Inter-Americana, 1942. (Another account of the life of Mme Lynch.)

Buzó Gomes, Sinforiano, ed., *Indice de la Poesía Paraguaya.* Asunción and Buenos Aires, Tupá, 1943.

Campos Cervera, Herib. *Ceniza Redimida.* Buenos Aires, Tupá, 1950. (Poems by a leading Paraguayan poet who died prematurely in 1953.)

Chaves, María Concepción Leyes de. *Madama Lynch.* Buenos Aires, Peuser, 1957. (A romanticized biography.)

—— *Tava'i.* Asunción, La Colmena, 1942. (A Paraguayan novel.)

Dombrowski, Katharina von. *Land of Women.* New York and London, Putnam's, 1935. (A novel of the times of Solano López.)

Domínguez, Manuel. *El Alma de la Raza.* Asunción, Cándido Zamphirópolos, 1918. Buenos Aires, Ayachucho, 1946.

Bibliography

—— *El Paraguay, sus Grandezas y sus Glorias.* Buenos Aires, Ayacucho, 1946.

Ghiano, Juan Carlos. *Memorias de la Tierra Escarlata.* Formosa (Argentina), América-Sapucai, 1954. (Impressions of Paraguay by a young Argentine literary critic.)

González, J. Natalicio. *Solano López y Otros Ensayos.* Paris, Las Indias, 1926.

—— *Proceso y Formación de la Cultura Paraguaya.* Asunción and Buenos Aires, Guarania, 1938.

—— *El Paraguay y la Lucha por su Expresión.* Asunción, Guarania, 1945.

Henríquez-Ureña, Pedro. *Literary Currents in Hispanic America.* Cambridge, Mass., Harvard University Press, 1949. (An excellent cultural history of Latin America.)

Roa Bastos, Augusto. *El Trueno entre las Hojas.* Buenos Aires, Losada, 1953. (Short stories by a Paraguayan poet.)

—— *Son of Man.* London, Gollancz, 1965. (*Hijo de Hombre*, a saga of Paraguay, trs. by Rachel Caffyn.)

Rodríguez Alcalá, José, ed., *Antología Paraguaya.* Asunción, H. Kraus, 1911.

Shepard, E. Clarence. *Francia.* London, Bentley, 1851. ('A tale of the Revolution of Paraguay, from Authentic Sources', dedicated to Viscount Palmerston.)

Southey, Robert. *A Tale of Paraguay.* London, Longman's, 1825.

Urbieta Rojas, Pastor. *Estampas Paraguayas.* Buenos Aires, Difusam, 1942.

Varela, Héctor F. ['Orion']. *Elisa Lynch.* Buenos Aires, 'La Enciclopedia de la Intelectualidad Argentina', 1934. (A historical novel.)

Vitis, Michael A. de, ed., *Parnaso Paraguayo.* Barcelona, Maucci, 1924.

Voltaire. *Candide.* 1759.

Wey, Walter. *La Poesía Paraguaya; Historia de una Incógnita.* Trs. from the Portuguese by Haydée Lagomarsino and Gladys Torres. Montevideo Biblioteca Alfar, 1951.

White, Edward Lucas. *El Supremo.* New York, Dutton, 1934. (A good historical novel of Paraguay under Dr Francia.)

V. PARAGUAYAN ECONOMY

Barrail, Enrique. *Ferro Carril Central del Paraguay.* Asunción, El Arte, 1964. (A résumé of the history of the railway and of plans for its reorganization.)

Bertoni, Guillermo Tell. *Geografía Económica Nacional del Paraguay.* Asunción, Editorial Guaraní, 1940.

Fisher, Frederic R., and others. *Investment in Paraguay.* Washington, U.S. Department of Commerce, 1955. (A general economic survey of the country. Much more comprehensive than the title suggests.)

Instituto de Bienestar Rural. *Diez Años de Reforma Agraria con Stroessner, 1954–1964.* Asunción, 1964. (Contains the text of Law no. 852 on agrarian reform.)

McKechnie, A. C. *South America's Southern Six.* London, Federation of British Industries, 1963. (Contains a brief chapter on the Paraguayan economy.)

Ministerio de Agricultura y Ganadería. *Programa de 5 Años para el mejoramiento agrícola del Paraguay.* Asunción, 1962.

Presidencia de la República. *Mensaje del Excelentísimo Señor Presidente de la República. . . .* Asunción, 1964. (A comprehensive survey of the Government's achievements and plans.)

U.S. Embassy. *Alianza para el Progreso en el Paraguay.* Asunción, 1965.

INDEX

95

PRINTED IN GREAT BRITAIN
BY THE BROADWATER PRESS LIMITED
WELWYN GARDEN CITY, HERTS

DATE DUE

MAY 4 '87			
GAYLORD			PRINTED IN U.S.A.